Praise for *Ten Years* W9-BSR-067

"A thoughtful and inspiring book."

—Savannah Guthrie

"It's such a great book . . . there's a universal quality to these stories."

—Kathie Lee Gifford

"I thought the book was fabulous."

—Steve Harvey

"The book is filled with these great and wonderful reminders of the capacity of a human being to overcome incredible adversity. . . . A great, great, great reminder of a great country and a great people, and [Hoda] is one of them."

—Mike Huckabee

"Fantastic. It's a great book."

—Jimmy Fallon

"I love the book."

—Wendy Williams

"Really smart . . . This is a fantastic book . . . a riveting read."

—Piers Morgan

"Kotb's book, *Ten Years Later* (written with Jane Lorenzini), offers inspirational profiles of six people who have overcome adversity."

—*The New York Times*

"Inspirational."

—*USA Today*

"*Ten Years Later: Six People Who Faced Adversity and Transformed Their Lives* stands out as a wrenching, heartfelt inspiration to better yourself in 2013. . . . These stories could easily tip over into maudlin territory, but Kotb's journalistic skills and her co-author and pal Jane Lorenzini's voice keep the tone smart and gripping."

—Fastcompany.com

"Sobering and inspiring tales in their own right, Kotb's journalistic acumen makes this collection all the more moving."

—*Publishers Weekly*

"Amazing and inspiring stories."

—*Ladies' Home Journal*

"Remarkable."

—*Access Hollywood*

"Perfect for anyone who needs a boost."

—PBGLifestyle.com

ALSO BY HODA KOTB

Hoda: How I Survived War Zones, Bad Hair, Cancer, and Kathie Lee

TEN YEARS LATER

Six People Who Faced Adversity
and Transformed Their Lives

HODA KOTB

❖◆❖ WITH JANE LORENZINI ❖◆❖

Simon & Schuster Paperbacks
New York   London   Toronto   Sydney   New Delhi

Simon & Schuster Paperbacks
A Division of Simon & Schuster, Inc.
1230 Avenue of the Americas
New York, NY 10020

First Simon & Schuster trade paperback edition February 2014

SIMON & SCHUSTER PAPERBACKS and colophon are registered trademarks
of Simon & Schuster, Inc.

For information about special discounts for bulk purchases,
please contact Simon & Schuster Special Sales at 1-866-506-1949
or business@simonandschuster.com.

The Simon & Schuster Speakers Bureau can bring authors
to your live event. For more information or to book an event,
contact the Simon & Schuster Speakers Bureau at
1-866-248-3049 or visit our website at www.simonspeakers.com.

Designed by Akasha Archer

Manufactured in the United States of America

10 9 8 7 6 5 4 3 2 1

Library of Congress has cataloged the hardcover edition as follows:

Kotb, Hoda.
  Ten years later : six people who faced adversity and transformed their lives / Hoda
Kotb; with Jane Lorenzini. — First Simon & Schuster hardcover edition.
    p. cm.
1. Life change events—Psychological aspects. 2. Adjustment (Psychology) 3. Biography.
I. Lorenzini, Jane, author. II. Title.
  BF637.L53K68 2013
  155.2'40922—dc23
  2012042253

ISBN 978-1-4516-5603-9
ISBN 978-1-4516-5604-6 (pbk)
ISBN 978-1-4516-5605-3 (ebook)

To Sami, Abdel, Judi, and Jim

~

And for anyone who needs hope

CONTENTS

INTRODUCTION

Ever asked it? With your nose pressed up against a mental crystal ball, your eyes squinting and your heart pounding, have you ever asked:

What will happen if I . . . ?

Fill in the blank: *get a divorce, win the lottery, am diagnosed with cancer, quit my job, suddenly lose someone I love.*

We've all wondered about a what-if and wished for time's guidance. We want time to say to us, "Yep, you've made the right decision." Or "Everything's going to work out just fine." But (hmph!) time won't tell. Not until we take a first step. Time then takes over, slowly turning our what-ifs into realities. The days, months, and years eventually reveal, like a Polaroid, a clear picture of how significant events and decisions ultimately shape our lives.

From time to time, I'll look back through the personal journals I've scribbled in throughout my life, the keepers of my raw thoughts and emotions. The words poured forth after my dad died, when I went through a divorce, and after I was diagnosed with breast cancer. There are so many what-ifs scribbled on those pages. I was desperate to know whether one day I would feel happy again, that I would find love again, that I would survive. How intriguing to look back at those past fears now that I have the benefit of hindsight. It made me think, *What if I asked other people to take a look back at their greatest challenges with a decade's worth of perspective? What an interesting concept for a book*. Plenty of us, including me, have struggled to take a first step toward an uncertain future. We've all prayed for the patience required to heal our pain, one excruciating day at a time. We've all wondered, in our darkest hours, how life could possibly change for the better.

Ten Years Later is about the journey six extraordinary people take with time. Each has experienced a game-changing event—perhaps a life-threatening illness or a catastrophic personal loss. Some of the challenges will make you wonder how the person got through the next ten minutes. Others will make you think a lifetime wouldn't be enough to overcome the damage done. Following the game changer, you'll find out what steps (or missteps) each person took and how each has fared over the next ten years. Did her decision turn out to be wise? How did he navigate the pain? Has she truly changed? Throughout the book, Time curls its pointer finger, beckoning Curiosity, "Come with me. See where I took this life."

In my own life, I've had numerous personal and professional game changers. Some broke my heart, others made me braver. One of the earliest game changers happened along an interstate. In 1987, I was driving around the Southeast in my mom's car, looking for my first job out of college. I had a degree in communications from Virginia Tech and a twenty-minute videotape résumé. I bought a new green suit for the one interview I so ignorantly assumed it would take to land a television reporting job in Richmond, Virginia. Well, I was off by about six suits and a hundred TV market rankings. Richmond told me no. Memphis said no. Three nos from Birmingham. My résumé tape got ejected from VCR after VCR, and my one day on the road turned into eight, then nine, then ten. "No, sorry." The maddening cycle of ejection, rejection, and dejection started in Virginia and continued all the way down through the Florida panhandle. A total of twenty-seven news directors told me no. I was devastated. My dream of working in TV news was now looking more like a career in public relations. I turned the car around and headed north back toward Virginia. And then, somewhere in Mississippi, I took a wrong turn. GPS systems and cell phones did not exist; I was officially lost. As I drove around looking for a way to get back on track, I noticed a billboard for WXVT featuring the CBS Eye. The station was located in Greenville, a TV market I hadn't considered. I figured, *What do I have to lose?* I drove to Greenville, digging deep for one last shred of hope. That very day, Stan Sandroni was promoted from WXVT's sports director to news director, and he agreed to see me. In went my résumé tape, and out came the words I so desperately wanted to hear.

"Hoda, I like what I see."

My wrong turn turned out to be one of the best mistakes I've ever made. Stan hired me after nearly thirty other people would not. Gutting out the challenge of rejection paid off. That chance meeting would prove to be a game changer in my life.

Ten Years Later profiles six people who've faced a series of life's game changers and challenges—abuse, illness, addiction, grief, job loss. These people didn't just fight their way through adversity, they forged better lives because of the battle. Their journeys are measured in the very small steps that painstakingly result in change and the big, bold leaps of faith that launch dreams. The book is meant to inspire you, wow you, motivate you, and move you—and maybe even do all those things within the same chapter. In the pages ahead, the courageous people who share their life stories have done so in hopes of enriching yours—now or ten years later.

AMY BARNES

I've met plenty of inspiring women on the *Today* show's Joy Fit Club who've lost a significant amount of weight. But when Joy shared with me the profile of a particular club member, Amy Barnes, I knew she was special. In the short story Amy wrote about her journey, it was clear that her astounding 340-pound weight loss was not her proudest accomplishment. This woman wanted to share what she considered the more important message. She wanted people to know that she had shed and survived an even heavier burden.

◆━◆◆◆━◆

In the spring of 2001, twenty-seven-year-old Amy Barnes was working as a paralegal at the Anoka County Public Defender's Office, thirty miles north of Minneapolis. Her career was solid, but her personal life was vulnerable, not that Amy recognized it. There were too many distractions. She had two sons from different fathers, a cheating husband, and a hundred extra pounds on her five-feet-eight frame. On a sunny April day, Amy walked next door to the courthouse to pick up new client files. As she headed back to her office, a handsome man her age started up a conversation.

"It was his smile, it was his eyes, it was the way he smelled, it was his voice," Amy recalls. "He was just smooth. He was well groomed and very well spoken. This was in the midst of me finding out my husband was having an affair. I had low self-esteem, and all of a sudden this really hot guy is paying attention to me."

(We'll call "this guy" Robert throughout.)

"I had this stack of file folders in my hand and he asked if he could help carry them back," she recalls. "He was a gentleman and nice, so he helped carry them back, and he saw that I worked at the PD office."

The tall, well-built Robert asked Amy for her number. She told him no; she was not interested.

The next day at work, a huge bouquet arrived for Amy.

"There must have been two to three dozen red roses, and all the card said was, *Dinner?*"

Robert called right as the flowers arrived. "I told him, 'Thanks, but no.'"

He called Amy's office every day for a week. She finally said yes to lunch. Robert drove them in his luxury sedan to the Coon Rapids Dam Regional Park along the Mississippi River.

"He went into the trunk and pulled out a blanket and this huge picnic basket," she says, "and we had a picnic in the park. That was our first date."

Amy grew up just thirteen miles northwest of the park in Elk River, Minnesota. She describes her parents as hardworking and her upbringing as loving and middle-class. She and her younger sister were raised to go to church and to get an education. In 1992, Amy graduated from high school and enrolled for a year in a small Christian liberal arts university in Saint Paul. By nineteen, Amy had met and begun dating her first boyfriend. She then transferred to Saint Cloud State University in Saint Cloud on a golf scholarship. But in

1994, at twenty-one, Amy became pregnant, making her ineligible for the grant. She lost her funding and her boyfriend, who was not interested in a relationship with his new son, Marcus.

"He was twenty-five and told me he didn't want to be a dad. He said, 'I'm not ready to be a dad.' I told him that being a dad was not a matter of convenience," she says, "and you either choose all or nothing. And he said, 'I choose nothing.'"

Amy got a part-time job on campus and a full-time job as a single parent. Ten months later, she met her second boyfriend. Over the next two years, school, work, a relationship, and the baby kept Amy very busy. In May 1998, she graduated with honors from Saint Cloud with three degrees—a bachelor of arts in criminal justice, minority studies, and human relations. She walked across the stage carrying her diploma and nine months of baby beneath her black gown. She gave birth to her second son, Terrell, a month later. Amy spent the next two years working toward a master's degree and raising her sons with Terrell's father. In June 2000, she got an MA in psychology and a certificate of marriage; she wed Terrell's dad after dating him for six years. But soon after, trouble began. Amy says her parents clearly taught her right from wrong, but for some reason, she kept making bad decisions when it came to men.

"I found out he was having an affair," she says, "and we were married for less than a year."

Amy admits the affair was not a shock. She says the relationship was broken from the start. She describes her then-husband as a frequent drinker and herself as a pushover. He was an absentee partner, but she welcomed help with the boys whenever he came home. She'd also become obese, gaining seventy pounds with Marcus and another seventy with Terrell, who weighed nearly thirteen pounds when he was born. Plus, Amy had a history of bad relationships with food.

"I've been on a diet since I was fourteen. My mom has been on a diet since I can remember," she explains. "There was never a time that I wasn't taking a diet pill, that I wasn't trying some crazy diet."

At 335 pounds, Amy was not only physically heavy, she felt the weight of the world on her shoulders as a working mother of two. She separated from her husband in April 2001 and began kickboxing at a local gym in an effort to lose weight.

That same month, she crossed paths with Robert, who was paying a traffic ticket fine at the county courthouse. Amy would have no way of knowing what a high price she'd pay for agreeing to have lunch with him in the park. Their relationship progressed quickly. Within six months of their first date, Robert moved in with Amy and her six- and three-year-old sons. She was happy to have a family, of sorts, to nurture.

"God put me on earth to be a wife and a mom," she says. "There's nothing that brings me more joy."

Amy felt self-assured in her new relationship.

"I stopped going to the gym and we ate out a lot. He made me feel secure the way I looked already, so losing weight wasn't as much of a necessity at that point. It was, 'I love you just the way you are, just the way you look; you're absolutely perfect.'"

Over the next few months, Amy's weight began to grow and her world began to shrink. She wasn't troubled by either change.

"I know now looking back it was all a control thing," she says. "He would call me ten times a day. I'd say, 'Hey, I'm going out with my girlfriends this weekend,' and he would say, 'No, I really want to spend time with you.' Abusers slowly try to close you off from your friends and family, but you don't realize it when you're in it."

Within a year, Robert's reactions intensified. He questioned Amy's every move and motive.

"The mental and emotional abuse started. I don't really remember when it transitioned from 'I love you. You don't need to go to your mom's' to the name calling and the checking the caller ID and seeing that my mom called, and being insecure about what we talked about, or, 'Why were you on the phone with your mom for twenty-seven minutes?' He would check the logs and check the caller ID to see who called. Then it got to the point where he would escalate things and accuse me of talking to another man," she says. "He would actually get more mad if he didn't see any phone calls come in, because then it was me deleting evidence that I was talking to my mom, or a friend, or some other guy. He would say, 'I know you talked to somebody. Who did you talk to?' It got to the point where people stopped calling the house because they knew the repercussions that I would face just based on their two- or three-minute check-in phone call."

Marcus and Terrell became leery of the increasingly volatile Robert.

"They would walk away and go in their rooms," she says. "They would just kind of disappear."

Eventually, Robert's war of words gave way to more potent weapons. He began to use his fists. He fired the first salvo on a drive back from a funeral in Indiana. Robert and Amy dropped off his brothers in Minneapolis. When Robert got back into the car, he accused her of sleeping with one of his brothers, even though both had stayed with an aunt, not in the hotel with Robert and Amy.

"He literally, with a closed fist, punched me three or four times in the face," she remembers. "Then there was an 'I'm sorry.' A honeymoon stage, like, 'I'm sorry, I'll never do it again.' That honeymoon period was probably the longest, because it was the first time he hit me. It was probably two or three months. That was long. After that, a honeymoon period could last anywhere from two weeks to three days."

Robert rarely hit Amy in the face or arms, to avoid causing obvious bruising on her body. She recalls a day when Robert returned from a trip and became enraged when he found no calls logged on her cell phone. It sparked a particularly brutal beating.

"He hit me on the same leg for two hours. It was like him hitting a punching bag. Every single time I said, 'I didn't talk to anyone,' he would hit me. He would rest from hitting me and move on to the name calling, the name calling, the name calling, and then he would start back in on my leg. It was so bad the next day that when I got out of bed, when I stepped on the ground, I collapsed onto the floor," she describes. "My leg was so swollen that I couldn't wear pants. My pants didn't fit on that side, so I had to wear a skirt."

I ask her if she ever tried to leave the room during the two hours.

"Ha. No. When he first hit me, I got up off the bed and I said, 'That hurt. Stop.' He yelled, 'Sit the F down.' The way he said it, I just listened. Because I'm thinking, *If I don't, it's just going to be worse. So I'll just sit down and it won't be as bad.* There were three other times during that tirade that I tried to get up," she says, "and the second time he screamed at me, and the third time he grabbed me by the back of the hair, pulled me back onto the bed, and told me not to get up again. A lot of people ask people in abusive relationships, 'Why do you put up with it? Why do you stay?' And it's because you can prepare yourself. You can mentally and emotionally and physically prepare yourself, and you always think that if you don't go along with what they're doing or saying, it's just going to be worse. So, if you can just calm them down and pacify them by doing whatever they want, or saying what they want to hear . . . You're willing to do anything just to make them stop."

Amy had four academic degrees, two little boys, and zero self-worth. Despite the abuse, she stayed with Robert.

"He has done everything from throwing a punch, a kick, he has strangled me, he has burned me with cigarettes," she says. "But I think the worst of everything that he has ever done—and I think a lot of women who have gone through domestic violence would also say this—is the emotional and mental abuse. He would get physically tired from beating me, so a beating could last ten minutes or a half an hour. But the name calling and the words that stung, that could last three or four hours. The worst thing—beyond the name calling for hours at a time—that he did all the time was spit in my face. That to me is the most disrespectful." She pauses. "I can't even explain it. I would have rather had him punch me in the face than spit on me."

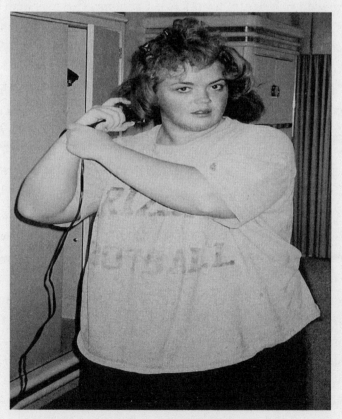

Amy at 395 pounds in 2003. Anoka, Minnesota.
(Courtesy of Amy Barnes)

Amy hated herself and her life, which had spun out of control. Her crutch and comfort was food. If an entire large pizza felt good, a whole ice cream cake for dessert felt even better. Amy gorged herself in the bathroom with the door shut or loaded up at the drive-through.

"I ate a lot in my car," she says, "or I ate a lot when Robert was gone or the kids were in bed."

Robert spent several days at a time away from home for work. Amy knew some of his relatives were involved with drugs but did not think Robert was, until one afternoon when she forgot her lunch and drove the two miles from work to eat at home. Her sons were in day care. Even from the garage, she could detect an overwhelming and unfamiliar smell. Amy walked into the kitchen and saw Robert and two of his relatives sitting at the breakfast counter.

"I'll never forget looking at the counter, and there was a sheet of newspaper, and it had a mound of white powder on it and I knew it was cocaine," she says. "That was the smell. They were cooking crack."

A horrified Amy says she "lost it."

"First of all, I worked at the public defender's office, and I had heard and seen what happens to people who are caught with drugs. Plus, if it's in my house, they could take my kids away. I screamed, 'What are you doing?!' I ran to the counter and I picked up the piece of paper and started running across the kitchen and up the stairs. I was three-hundred-plus pounds. The powder is blowing off the paper. I went running up the stairs, and he's running after me, and right when I got to the bathroom, I did this"—she tilts the imaginary sheet of newspaper downward—"into the toilet. I did it without thinking of the ramifications. My whole thing was, *If someone finds this, they could take my kids away. I could go to prison.* It was all over the place. I can still see the look on his face."

One relative followed Robert up to the bathroom and began screaming at her.

"Robert grabbed me by the back of the hair and was beating me on the bathroom floor."

The other relative bounded up the stairs and told Robert, "That's enough."

Amy says she doesn't know the exact street value of the cocaine she dumped into the toilet, but she did feel that had his relative not intervened, Robert was enraged enough to have killed her.

To her knowledge, Robert never again brought drugs into the house. Amy admits to making poor decisions of her own during the relationship with Robert. She says she did things with him and for him that were against her principles.

"Honestly, when I was with him, I was an ugly person; he made me an ugly person. I became a very negative and hateful person, and that's not who I am. I don't deny anything I ever did that I'm not proud of, but I was a product of my environment."

Things got very ugly. The pattern of violence was reinforced month after month and year after year. Robert did not abuse Marcus or Terrell; he saved his cruelty for Amy. She would take the abuse until she reached a breaking point and then leave. She and the boys would show up repeatedly at her parents' house. Despite their horror, Amy says they never turned their backs on her.

"I came home two, three, or four A.M. and I had a bloody face, and I was bruised, and my mom took a picture of me and said, 'This is what he's doing to you and your family and your kids!' and I literally didn't care," Amy says, describing her state of mind. "You're not hearing what they're saying. My mom said, 'You have a choice at this point. It's gonna be you or your kids.' At that point, I was like, 'F you, Mom, you can't tell me what to do, I'm grown!' Two hours later, Robert is calling me and begging and crying and saying, 'Baby, I'm sorry, I promise I'll get help.' My mom and I would get in screaming fights. She would beg me, 'If you want to go back to that nonsense, leave my grandbabies here.' I was blessed to have my parents, as much as I'm sure they wanted to kill me, because every time I'd knock on their door at three o'clock in the morning bloodied and bruised, and say that me and my kids needed a place to stay, two days later, they'd watch me walk out of their house with the same person who did that to us."

The pain of watching that pattern runs so deep for Amy's mom and for Amy's closest friend, who also housed Amy several times, that neither wanted to share her memories of that time. It's a door they've closed and dead-bolted. Imagine the immeasurable frustration and fear they felt. Amy just kept going back, and taking the kids with her.

"He would beg and plead, 'I'll never do this again. We'll go to counseling,' all these broken promises. And I would go back. Every time. The person that is there is the person you love and has a great personality. You fell in love with Jekyll, but then when they abuse you, it's Hyde. But when they beg for you back, they put forward Jekyll, who you love and who made you feel special. It's a never-ending battle of abuse and the person you love, especially when you are two, three, four hundred pounds," she says. "Every time he came back to me he said, 'No one's gonna love you like me. No one's gonna love you because of the way you look. I'm the only one who's ever gonna love you because you're as fat as you are,' and I'd be thinking, *You're right; I'm four hundred pounds.*"

Amy felt hopeless and numb. She had big problems and little faith.

"I was raised in the church. I was confirmed. We went to church every week. But I turned from God. I was like, *If there really was a God, he would not have me going through this,*" she says. "I threw Bibles in the garbage. I threw crosses and crucifixes in the garbage, because I was sure there was not a God."

By the time Marcus and Terrell were seven and four years old, they were very afraid of Robert. Their mother's pattern of escaping his wrath became a routine part of their young lives.

"When we escaped in the middle of the night, Marcus knew to be quiet. Whenever I went into his room and woke him up at two o'clock in the morning, as a seven-year-old, he knew he needed to be quiet. He would put on his shoes without question; he knew that he was going to walk next to me," she says, "and we would walk into his brother's room, and his brother was only four, and I would pick my young son up, and at that time I was five hundred pounds, so here we were, trying to escape in the middle of the night."

Amy starts to cry, thinking about what she was asking of her little boys.

"Marcus would put on his shoes, and he would grab his jacket without making a sound so we could go wake Terrell. Even at four years old, Terrell would wake up and not cry. He would just grab his shoes, knowing we were trying to escape that night."

Amy had mapped out the quietest escape route before she ever needed to use it.

"The house we were in, the floors would creak. And because I was so heavy," she explains, "I would actually, when Robert was gone, get out of bed, and I would walk on the floor to find out where the boards creaked, so I could make an escape route where he wouldn't hear me. I knew the third and the seventh step I couldn't step on, because I was too heavy and that the floor would creak, and I would be too scared that he would wake up."

Amy's plan extended beyond the floorboards and out onto the street where her truck was parked.

"I knew how to pop a clutch without actually turning on the vehicle to get it started once I rolled down the hill, so he wouldn't hear us."

In early 2004, following a series of numbing episodes of abuse,

Amy woke up on a Sunday morning with an intense need to go to church.

"I didn't even believe in God at that point, because if there was a God I would not be going through what I'd been going through. But there was just an overwhelming feeling—I can't even explain it—that I needed to go to church," she says. "I didn't even know what church I would go to because I hadn't been to church in years."

Amy left the bed and went into the bathroom. When she began to shower, Robert woke up and asked her where she was going. She told him to church.

"So, of course, there was this extreme jealousy, like I was going to see someone. The next thing I remember is him pulling me out of the shower and beating me." She starts to cry, recalling how her youngest found her lying on the bathroom floor. "I woke up to my four-year-old son waking me up, scrubbing my face with the drenched bath mat, saying, 'Mama, wake up. I want to make you look beautiful again.'"

Amy never made it to church, but she did make up her mind.

"I was like, *That's it. I cannot be here anymore.*"

When Robert left the house, Amy packed as much as she could into her truck and, with her parents' support, hit the road. She and the boys moved in with girlfriends who lived in Madison, Wisconsin. Before long, she found a town house and created a more peaceful setting for herself and her sons.

Three months later, the doorbell rang at midnight.

"And I opened the door and he was standing there," she says. "The sense of fear and urgency—I can't even explain the feeling. He was crying and begging and 'I'm sorry, I came to find you,' and 'I can't live without you,' and all the things abusers do to get you back. They feed on your insecurities and all the things that they've been priming you for during the years that you've been in this ridiculous relationship."

Amy wanted desperately to believe Dr. Jekyll, standing on her doorstep.

"The person that comes back to you—and this is with every abusive relationship—and begs for your forgiveness and begs for you to come back to them is the person you fell in love with. It's this kind person who is smart and gorgeous and affectionate. And he is standing on the opposite side of the doorway."

Robert told Amy he'd enrolled in anger management classes and that he loved her. But Amy squared up to Robert and beat back the kernel of hope she felt forming in her heart.

"I was like, 'Screw off. I'm not taking you back.'"

Robert didn't give up. Every weekend, he drove the four hours from Minnesota to Wisconsin to see her. He showed her the certificate he got from attending anger management classes. He reminded Amy of his difficult childhood—raised by a crack-addicted and physically abused mother who suffered a fatal heart attack in front of him—claiming she, Amy, was all he had.

I hate to even ask Amy if she took him back, but I do.

"Of course. A complete dumbass. I was a complete dumbass," she admits.

In mid-2004, she and the boys moved back to Minnesota into Robert's house. Two weeks later, Amy needed to drive back to Wisconsin to put her house on the market. The kids had to go to school, so she left them with Robert. The honeymoon period was in full effect.

"It was the person I fell in love with," she says. "He was wonderful with me; he was wonderful with the kids."

Amy returned from her trip on a Monday, and asked Robert to go with her to pick up the boys, now eight and five years old, from school.

"I get to the school, and the principal says to me, 'I can't give

you any information about your kids; you have to call social services.'"

Confused, Amy got back in the car with Robert and called her
mom.

"She said, 'Are you with Robert?' and I told her yes. She said,
'You have a custody hearing on Thursday morning at eight thirty
because your kids were beaten very badly. And because you were
out of state, the state gave your dad and me temporary custody of
the boys.'"

The situation that sparked the abuse occurred while the boys
were staying by themselves with Robert. He found laundry on the
floor, became angry, and went after Terrell. When Marcus came to
his brother's defense, Robert beat them both. The boys showed up
for school with welts and bruises on their bodies caused by Robert's blows with a cable cord. Ultimately charges were filed against
Robert for beating the boys.

Amy was shocked by her mother's words. *Your kids were beaten
very badly.* She was infuriated. The usual nausea she felt before a
confrontation with Robert was replaced by focused rage. Amy turned
toward him, still holding the phone.

"I was in the car with him and I looked at him and I said, 'You
beat my kids?' For him to see that anger and fear in my face, he
must have worried that he was going to lose control of me. He
took the phone while I was still on with my mom and threw it out
the window. My mom said she thought that was the last time she
would ever hear my voice. And he said, 'I did not beat your children. I disciplined them, and if you have any lack of understanding
between the two, I will show you the difference between discipline
and a beating.'"

And he did. He drove Amy home and beat her for the next three
days.

"I had no concept of time. I couldn't see because my eyes were swollen shut. And when you black out from being beaten, you don't know if you've blacked out for two minutes or two days. My only concept of time was what I could hear on the TV. Robert was so physically exhausted from beating me, he would fall asleep. But before he did, he would shackle me to him. And when you're almost five hundred pounds, there is nothing you can do gracefully or quietly. I had lost blood, I hadn't eaten, I had urinated on myself; I was a mess. But I knew at that point I had to get to that hearing in court."

Amy says when she heard late-night talk show host Conan O'Brien's voice on television on what she guessed was the third night, she knew she didn't have very much time left to get to the eight thirty A.M. hearing.

"I literally got on my knees," she says, beginning to cry, "and I said, 'God, I know that this is my time, and I am asking your forgiveness, because it's either me or him. Either I am going to kill him and ask your forgiveness and that you take my soul to heaven, or he's going to kill me, and I need you to take care of my kids and take my soul.' I was mentally prepared to kill him, still shackled to him, so I could get away from him and get to my kids."

When Amy attempted to free herself from Robert, he woke up and was enraged.

"I was at the point where I was done. I didn't care anymore. The only thing that had kept me alive for the past two or three years was my kids. If it wasn't for my kids, I wouldn't have cared if he killed me. Abusers take your soul from you. You have no soul."

Robert and Amy's toxic three-year relationship had come down to a death match.

"I said to him, 'It's me or you.' And he said, 'It's not gonna be me,'" she says. "The next thing I remember is him stabbing me with a knife in the center of my stomach, and everything went black."

When she came to, Amy heard sirens blaring and voices asking her questions.

"I had no ID, nobody knew who I was," she says. "I was just this fat, bloodied, abused person lying on the sidewalk in front of the courthouse. To this day, I do not know for sure how I got there."

Emergency workers in front of the Sherburne County courthouse were trying to get a handle on the identity of the beaten, bleeding woman. Amy was trying to get answers about the date and time.

"I'm like, 'What day is it? What day is it?' And they said, 'It's Thursday. Who did this to you?' I told them and said they needed to bring me to my kids," she says. "They said, 'Ma'am, you're in critical condition.' I told them I didn't care, and I blacked out. Everything went black."

Amy says emergency workers later told her that they lost her heartbeat for a few seconds. They managed to stabilize her and get her into the ambulance. She continued to tell them she needed to go to court, but they insisted that she go instead to the hospital.

"I said, 'You cannot legally keep me here and I have to get to my kids.' There was a cop who told the EMTs they couldn't legally take me, even though I was in critical condition. So, they wheeled me to court on a stretcher, covered with a sheet because I was naked, and they stabilized me with tubes. I will never forget the look on my father's face," she says, breaking down, "but I looked at the judge and I said, 'I just want my kids back.'" She continues through tears. "And the judge said, 'You have to get healthy for them.' The judge didn't care that I was five hundred pounds. The judge didn't care that I was fat. He was saying, in order for you to get your kids back, you have to be mentally and emotionally healthy. It wasn't about me getting physically healthy, it was mentally and emotionally. I was a freakin' basket case because of all the stuff I was going through. And honestly, at that point in my life, I didn't care if I lived or died, but my kids are the reason I breathe. The judge said, 'In order to get your kids back, you have to get a job, you have to find a place to live, you have to pass assessments by the state.'"

The ambulance took Amy to the hospital, where representatives from a local battered women's shelter told her they had a bed waiting for her if she wanted it. She told them to save it for her.

Once Amy was released from the hospital, she entered the shelter, the Alexandra House. She took advantage of pro bono legal work offered at the shelter and filed an order for protection against Robert. She also divorced her estranged husband. Amy wanted a clean slate and, first and foremost, her boys back. Amy immediately began looking for a job.

"The judge said to me I needed to have a job, and I didn't care if it was at 7-Eleven; I needed to get my kids back," she says.

Amy applied for any and all jobs. She got a call back from a software company to interview for a position as an executive assistant and a paralegal.

"I was black and blue when I went to the job interview. My eyes were swollen shut, I had stitches in my body; I was a hot mess. The guy asked me, 'What would be your availability?' and I said, 'I'm not leaving here without a job.'" Amy pauses, crying. "And he gave me a job. And that was the only thing I needed, was for someone to be able to believe in me enough to work so I could get my kids back."

The job paid her bills, which led to an apartment and a car. In August, Amy threw a party for Marcus's ninth birthday and to celebrate their upcoming reunion as a family. In September, Amy's hard-earned dream came true: she got full custody of her sons after a trying four months. All three continued counseling to deal with what they'd endured over the years at the hands—and mouth—of Robert.

"I lived in fear of him. I always looked over my shoulder. The counselors gave the kids whistles for around their necks to express their fears. So, anytime they saw something that reminded them of him, like his sedan," she explains, "they would blow the whistle. If they heard a song that reminded them of Robert, they would blow the whistle. That was their security."

Ultimately, Robert pled to lesser charges arising from the incidents in May and spent a few months in jail. Still, Amy's peace of mind was rattled by the relentless ringing of her cell phone. Robert's calls were a violation of the protective order against him. He even called Amy during the few months he spent in jail.

"Each time he called my cell phone, I called the police, and they would file an order-for-protection violation," she says. "The Plymouth police department already had pre-filled-out police reports because they knew they were going to have to come out and see me, because I was going to call them to file an order-for-protection violation. They wouldn't have to fill out my name and address; they'd just fill in the time that he called and the number that he called from."

At some point, Amy said she'd simply had enough. *Ring-ring!*

"I looked at my phone and I saw his number come in, and I pushed *talk* on my cell phone. And I think he was just as surprised as I was that I answered," she says. "I could hear he was there. I was so angry and filled with hate, but I actually felt sorry for him, because I knew him as a person, and there is a legitimately good side of him, and he's had a horrible life as a child, which is not an excuse, but he doesn't know anything different. So I said, 'I have forgiven you for what you did to me and my kids, and you have no control over me anymore.' There was dead silence, and it felt like an eternity, and he hung up. And I have never heard from him since then. When they know that they don't have control, they don't want you anymore."

But Amy wanted a lot more. She had finally rid herself of Robert and had earned back her kids. The counseling had helped her realize the depth of her battered psyche; she was diagnosed with post-traumatic stress disorder. Amy wanted to be mentally and physically healthy for her boys, so she began to implement what she already knew from decades of experience.

"I've done Weight Watchers, the cabbage soup diet, I did Atkins for a while, I did just exercise and diet pills, I did the Zone Diet, I did Nutrisystem, I did prescription appetite suppression pills," she says. "Fat people are the smartest people when it comes to dieting because we have read every book, we have been on every diet, we have tried every pill; so fat people are super smart when it comes to dieting. We know what to do. We know what we're supposed to eat; we know what we're not supposed to eat. We know we're supposed to eat lean proteins and healthy carbs and lots of veggies, lots of water, but people don't address the root cause as to why they're fat in the first place. So, I knew what to do as far as what I was supposed to do physically. But going to counseling at that time was key, because it was addressing the root cause as to why I used food as an addiction. Most people use alcohol or drugs, but most people don't recognize food as an addiction like crack or alcohol."

Amy knew she needed to develop a sound eating plan that she could follow the rest of her life.

"I just kind of incorporated all the diets I liked," she says. "I wanted it to be sustainable. And then, ninety-eight percent of it was portion control."

Amy knew she also needed to sweat. At 490 pounds, she was embarrassed to begin working out in a gym. She decided to start moving to Billy Blanks Tae Bo fitness VHS tapes in her living room, and to walk around the block. Once. Amy literally took it one step at a time.

I ask her how long it took before exercise felt a bit easier.

"Oh, my God. Ha! Probably six months. The first week I went three times around the block, so each week I had a new goal. I would either walk two times around or I would go one time around, but it had to be faster than the week prior. So, if it took me an hour the first week, the next had to be under fifty-nine minutes. Every week there was a goal for either duration or time. Even with Tae Bo, I would only add a minute. It wasn't like, *Oh, I'm feeling great this week, I'm gonna do twenty minutes.* I set realistic goals."

In nine months, Amy lost a hundred pounds. She rewarded herself with a membership to the Anoka YMCA, undeterred by judging eyes.

"Sometimes people would look," she says, "but people stared at me when I was five hundred pounds, so people staring at me now was not any different."

Amy focused on using the Nautilus and cardio machines but avoided the group fitness classes. She drew the line there for bravery.

"You're freaked out. You're way too scared to do that in front of everybody."

Amy continued working on her health and working at the software company that had taken a chance on her. She was also busy raising Marcus and Terrell. As sore as her body was, Amy says the tougher challenge was mental.

"There are just days that suck going to the gym. You've had a long day at work, you're tired, you have stuff to do, there are groceries to get, the house is dirty, and so there are always roadblocks. You can use every excuse in the book not to go. So I think for me, it was more mental—mentally getting through the excuses."

Excited for her fresh start, Amy's coworkers took it upon themselves to create online profiles for her on two dating websites. In

March 2006, Amy met a man named Daryl Barnes over the Internet. He lived in Virginia and worked in Washington, D.C. She admits now that it was too soon, but Amy moved her family from Minnesota to Virginia to live with Daryl after knowing him for just three months. She loved the idea of a new beginning.

"I was starting from scratch—from the gym, to people, to my job, to everything."

Before she moved, she landed a job in D.C. with the Gates Foundation, supporting directors involved with improving education in the United States. She also joined Gold's Gym. She and Daryl were married in June 2007 and amicably divorced in July 2008. She kept his last name and calls him a good man. They both simply moved forward too quickly.

Amy's quest for fitness and health continued. She now weighed 240 pounds and began to experiment with equipment that would reshape her body.

"I was using free weights and doing group fitness classes, because they helped with the weight loss and there was a sense of accountability. Gold's Gym is more of a muscle-head gym, so that was my first taste of seeing bodybuilders and people in the fitness industry work out," she explains. "That's when I was like, *Yep, that's what I want to do; that's how I want to look.* And, even though I was heavier, I worked out on the free weights and nobody ever questioned it or made me feel uncomfortable. Sometimes, someone would ask me, and I'd say, 'I want to be a bodybuilder,' and there I was at 220 pounds, and they would just say, 'Okay, good for you.'"

Amy worked out at four thirty in the morning before heading to the office. She always saw a fellow early bird there named Allen Thompson, who worked at the Pentagon. They shared an interest in health and fitness, and eventually began dating.

"Here was this person who was strong, and driven, and passionate about everything," says Allen. "She was passionate about the way she cooks, and passionate about her dogs, passionate about her kids, and I liked that."

When her weight dropped to two hundred pounds, Amy studied for and received certification as a personal trainer. She added to that a certification in nutrition. More and more, Amy realized her interest and passion lay in sharing all she'd learned about domestic violence and overall health. Amy quit her job at the Gates Foundation and established her own health and fitness company. In November 2009, she and Allen competed in an international fitness competition in Fort Lauderdale, Florida. Over four years, she had lost an astounding 325 pounds.

"I actually took a picture on my phone," she says. "I weighed in at that competition at one-sixty-nine."

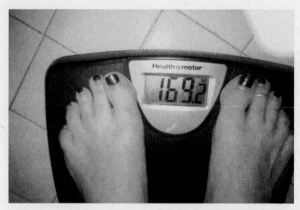

Weight at 2009 FAME International Championships.
Ft. Lauderdale, Florida. (Courtesy of Amy Barnes)

(In case you're wondering, I asked Amy why she doesn't have issues with excess skin, which can be a side effect from extensive weight loss. She says she does have extra skin, but in bodybuilding photos, she wears sheer pants or a wrap to cover her legs and belly area. She says there are other factors that reduced her extra-skin issue.

"For me, it's because of good genetics. Secondly, I was in my early to midthirties when I was at my heaviest. Thirdly, it's because I lost the weight slowly, and because I lifted weights. Even when I was heavy, I lifted weights the whole time.")

In 2009, Amy also became a contractor with the Department of Labor and began working with kids enrolled in the Job Corps program. Her role was to head up the Health and Wellness program, but it was also a chance for Amy to encourage underprivileged kids and to share with them what she'd learned by living through domestic violence.

"The weight loss to me is the most secondary part of my life," she says, "in comparison to everything else my kids and I have been through."

Allen has heard some but not all of what Amy endured during her years with Robert. He says she takes responsibility for her role in the situation and has been extremely open about the rawness of the abuse.

"It's hard. It makes me angry, but at the same time, it puts the day-to-day stuff into perspective. I thought *I* had baggage; I don't have any baggage. I thought *I* had some drama; I haven't been through anything," he says. "It changes your outlook on life. The guys at work ask me all the time, 'Why are you so, like, 'It's getting better, just take baby steps,' and I just say, 'Because I live with somebody who has survived the unimaginable, and then figured out a way to get her kids back, and raised two kids who are great young men.' It's humbling."

Amy exposes the Job Corps kids she works with to opportunities in the fitness industry and encourages them to excel. Many have neglectful parents and live in broken homes.

"To them, domestic violence is normal. I see these kids and I just want to rescue every single one of them. These kids have never had anybody believe in them. It's sad, because that's all they know; they wouldn't know a healthy relationship if it bit 'em in the ass. My kids could have turned out like these Job Corps kids, but they didn't. They are straight-A students; they are part of the football team. Everything they've been through has somehow made them better kids, and better human beings, and more accepting of people and adversity. They get being poor, they get not having anything, they get being teased because you're fat or you're a mixed race. The adversity could have turned them to drugs and to being hoodlums, but they have turned out to be law-abiding citizens and the coolest kids you'll ever meet." She starts to cry. "Because they are strong and they are kind. My kids and I have a very special relationship. I want them to be proud of me and they want me to be proud of them. And Allen has been a strong male role model for them now for four years."

From the start, Amy told Allen she wanted him to influence her sons in a positive way and to be involved in disciplining them. As you might imagine, that took some finesse.

"There were a few times when Marcus would come to protect his brother because he thought that I was going to do something to him," says Allen, "that I was going to hurt him because I was yelling at him about his grades. It just took a while for them to realize that I was in a position that I wanted them to be great, just like their mom. Once we got to the understanding that I wasn't gonna put my hands on them and hurt them, we were great. It wasn't hard, we just needed time."

Marcus and Terrell watched closely how Allen treated Amy.

"Marcus would do the same thing with his mom; he'd come check on her. Once they were able to see that we could have a disagreement and still be okay, and no one was physically harmed, and that we could have disagreements as adults, then they could trust me."

By 2010, work and home life for Amy were busy and productive, but it was time for another move. The D.C. area was too expensive and warm days were too rare. Amy, her sons, and Allen headed for the sunny South.

TEN YEARS LATER

In July 2011, with fifteen hundred miles and ten years between Amy and the day she met Robert, a new chapter began for her in Orlando, Florida. Marcus and Terrell, fifteen and thirteen, settled into school and joined the track and football teams. Allen found work similar to his role at the Pentagon, but in the private sector. Amy took a job at a women's fitness studio as a weight-loss consultant and manager but decided a year later to work fewer hours and for herself. In March 2012, she started a new venture, creating custom weight-loss programs for clients.

At thirty-eight, Amy is tanned and pretty. All totaled, she wears five rings on her fingers, which are tipped with a French manicure. Her built arms are a testament to her dedication in the gym. Amy's shoulder-length hair is dark, her eyes are hazel, and she is open, funny, and straightforward. A typical day for her begins before sunrise.

"Our alarm goes off every morning at four thirty, we both start with a protein shake, and we share a cup of coffee on the way to the gym," she says, referring to Allen. "We work out at the gym upwards of an hour and a half to two hours. We lift a particular body part, we usually do some kind of boxing circuit, and then we'll do cardio for thirty or forty-five minutes. Then, I come home and I eat breakfast, which usually consists of egg whites and oatmeal, and then my day starts."

Amy prepacks her lunch, usually lean protein and veggies, nothing with enriched white flour. She eats every two to three hours—perhaps brown rice or a sweet potato, sometimes vegetables. In the middle of the day, she fixes another protein shake. Some days she works as a consultant at doctors' offices, other days she spends time answering e-mails, marketing her company, or writing articles for two fitness magazines.

"My days usually end at four o'clock, because I go and pick up my kids from school." She adds, "I have to say, as old as they are, could they walk home? Sure."

But Amy says that's why she started her own business. The flexibility adds to her quality of life.

"I get to pick them up from school, and I get to go to their track meets and their football games, and to me, that's more important than having to work seventy hours a week just to pay the bills."

The brothers are close. Marcus is a junior in high school, is a European history buff, and plays center on the varsity football team. Terrell is in eighth grade and runs the mile in track.

Evenings mean cooking dinner, taking care of the dogs, helping with homework, and doing laundry.

"There are some times," she says, laughing, "I'll look at Allen and say, 'Is it too early to go to bed?' And he's like, 'Honey, it's six forty-five.' We're typically in bed by eight thirty or nine o'clock."

Amy's life now is a far cry from her former life. She says the topic of those dark days almost never comes up. Her parents never bring it up, nor do her sons. Both boys declined an interview. Amy recalls a rare moment when Marcus referenced their old life.

"He made a comment like, 'You know that Terrell and I are old enough now that we will always protect you.' Because at ten and seven," she says, "they couldn't."

I ask her if she ever worries about falling back into unhealthy or destructive habits.

Keynote speaker at 2010 women's health expo.
Fredericksburg, Virginia. (Courtesy of Amy Barnes)

"No. I don't use food as a coping mechanism anymore. I eat because food is what I need to live. Me working out and me living
a healthy lifestyle is like me brushing my teeth," she says. "As far
as the abuse goes, I think I went through it so I can show other
people what it is. Emotional and mental abuse is control. And when
you think your husband or your boyfriend is being super caring or
super sensitive and he is calling your phone—especially these young
girls—they're calling or texting you fifteen times a day, or they don't
want you to hang out with your friends because they'd rather spend
time with you, and they don't want you with your friends and family because they just want you all to themselves because they love
you, that is the first telltale sign of emotional abuse. They're trying

to control you. And from there, it escalates. So, I had to go through it to recognize it, so I can help and coach other people through it."

Amy travels for speaking engagements to encourage and enlighten women like her, who have survived domestic abuse.

"I can't speak to the victims who are buried, because they couldn't get out of it. Every time I speak, it's to the survivors, and I say, 'I applaud you for finally taking the leap to get out,' but to the victims who are still stuck and can't find a way out, the thing I tell them is, 'The unknown is scary, because when you're in it, you know what to expect, and you can brace yourself for the abuse. You can make excuses and try to make things better. But the unknown is scary, because you don't know what you'll do financially. They have excluded you from finding a job and having financial stability, and isolated you from family and friends, and at this point you feel you have nothing in your life. The unknown is scary, because if you leave him, what the F are you gonna have? Nothing. No money, no friends, no family, no job, no security, no nothin'.' But I tell them, 'The unknown is scary, but being in what you are with him is so much F-ing scarier than the unknown.'"

I ask Amy if *she* would have braved the unknown had it not been for a judge ordering her to better her life.

"No. No, because that judge forced me to say, *It is him or your children.* I went through three years with this guy, back and forth with him every week, every month. I went through this craziness. It was the abuse, it was the honeymoon period, it was the abuse again, it was the honeymoon period," she says. "I left and came back into that relationship over those three years so many times, and it was never bad enough."

We talk about the residue from the bad years and what remains.

"I have a five-inch scar up the center of my stomach from where he stabbed me. I have scars from when he has burned me with cigarettes, from where he has cut me with a razor blade. The bruises have healed, but those emotional scars and mental scars affect me more now, even ten years later, than any of those other scars ever did," she says. "Just like the physical scars will never go away, I will always have them."

In Amy's work as a weight-loss consultant, her past serves as a guidebook in her sessions with obese clients.

"There's a purpose for everybody. I feel like all that stuff that I had to go through had a purpose. I coach and counsel people now and I help them get healthy. When you're living an unhealthy life, there's nobody who can tell you there's a better side, unless there's somebody who's actually been to the other side to show you there's a way out. When there's a client sitting in front of me who's four hundred pounds, there's an underlying reason why. I understand it. I've been there," she says. "Not only do I have the certificates and the credentials and the book smarts, but I have some clout to back it up, because I lived it and I breathed it and I dreamed it. I think it gives me credibility with people because they think, *She understands what I'm going through*."

For Amy, the quickest and most effective way to help people is to get to the heart of the matter. She feels like she's earned the right to be frank.

"I ask them, 'Why are you fat?' I use the F-word all the time, because I've been there. Until you acknowledge why you are over-weight, and why you use food as an addiction, and why you use food to cope, you will never, ever, ever be cured," she says, "and I tell people that. 'Why are you at three hundred pounds? What's going on in your life?' It's abuse, it's a bad marriage, it's a bad job, it's bad kids—there's a thousand and one reasons why people are three, four, five hundred pounds. It's not because they want to be fat and gluttonous, it's because there's something super, super messed up in their lives that is causing them to use food as a coping mechanism, just like a crackhead, or a drug addict, or an alcoholic would."

There is a sense of relief for Amy in knowing that there was a reason for the brutal challenges she faced in her life. From her own darkness, she can now shed light on a solution for someone else.

"I can't tell you how many people I've had say to me, 'I need you to save my wife's life.' Or there's a mom standing there with her four-hundred-pound son and she says, 'I need you to save my son's life.' That's a lot to ask of somebody. I'm not God, but those opportunities have been presented to me every day for the last two-plus years, and I view every one of those opportunities as a gift, because that's why I'm here. I can't promise you that I'm going to save your life, but I can give you every tool that I've ever had to try to help you," she says, "and that is what I'll be doing until the day I die."

Amy wants to spread her message of getting healthy both on the inside and out. She's clearly worked hard, and painstakingly, for overall strength in her own life. She wants others to see in her journey the power inherent in taking that first step toward change.

"I think I finally found my purpose. My purpose is to be a motivational speaker and a life coach. And my life is fucked up," she says with a laugh, "but I think I've been through enough to be able to understand people's fucked-up lives. To be able to motivate and inspire people. I had to go through all of that in order to be able to do what I do. People can think, *She went through all of that? Then I know that I can do it.* I would go through it all over again if that meant that I could save a person's life from domestic violence or obesity. I am now supposed to coach and counsel and mentor people to finally live the life that they're supposed to."

The relief Amy feels about finding her purpose in life resonates in these words from Mark Twain. I came across them after I met Amy. They made me think of her.

"The two most important days in your life are the day you are born, and the day you find out why."

Amy Barnes was born on November 10, 1973. It took her years of beatings, losing her children, and 490 pounds to find out why.

LINDSAY BECK

So many of us know people who've battled a medical crisis, or we ourselves have endured one. When WebMD ran its magazine's annual "Health Heroes" section in 2006, a small blurb about a young woman named Lindsay Beck packed a big wow factor. Lindsay had accomplished so much. Never did we think we'd find someone who, at age thirty-five, already had a fascinating ten-years-later tale to share. But Lindsay does. And oddly enough, her story has an intimate connection with an NBC colleague whom I know and love.

———◆———

When you meet Lindsay Beck for the first time, you feel like you've met her before. She's got that kind of face. An effortless white smile, fresh skin, a chestnut ponytail, and blue-green eyes that make you close yours. *Hmm. Did I buy peaches from her at the farmers' market? Was she in that Ivory soap commercial?* Lindsay is a thirty-five-year-old who looks twentysomething, burdened by nothing. Well, ha. What a joke. If the inside of Lindsay's body could read that description, it would laugh. It would throw back its formerly ravaged, toxic head and snicker at the words. A C-shaped scar on Lindsay's neck is the trapdoor to her medical past. When you lift it, you see two rival stories: a double helix of dark and light.

The San Francisco Bay suburbs where Lindsay grew up are now some of the most expensive zip codes in the country. But back in 1976, when she was born, the dot-coms and their megamillions were nonexistent. Merrilee and Michael Nohr, Lindsay's parents, fell in love in high school, got married, and soon realized they were not meant to be together. They divorced when Lindsay was four and her brother was just one. Her mother soon became involved with the father of Lindsay's best friend from preschool. The dream that little girls have of becoming sisters with their closest friend came true. Her new stepdad, Bob, also had a second daughter, so a blended family of six was formed. Lindsay describes her childhood as "vanilla."

"Not in a bad way," she explains. "It was safe, full of sports, school, family, and a sense of community."

The divorce did create some challenges every other weekend. That's when Lindsay and her brother would stay with their father, who had not yet embarked on his two future marriages.

"My mom would say, 'Here's the toothbrushes, here's the clothes, you're in charge,'" recalls Lindsay. "But my dad was a bachelor, so I can remember calling my mom and saying, 'Dad has no food; we're eating ice. But don't worry, I'm making sure everything's okay.'"

The bulk of Lindsay's family life was consistent and loving, filled with swim meets, soccer games, and trips to the beach. Her mom and dad did not go to college, but Bob did. He felt strongly that Lindsay should, too. When it was time to choose a school, Bob guided Lindsay away from the California university where her high school friends and boyfriend were headed, and toward the University of Colorado in Boulder.

"Bob sat me down and said, 'The choice is yours, but this is a mistake you'll regret the rest of your life. At Boulder, they have study-abroad programs, you'll meet all new people, and the opportunities there are enormous. If you follow your friends, where is that going to get you?'"

Lindsay listened and Bob was right. Her roommates were from Minnesota, Mississippi, Louisiana, and Ohio, and as Lindsay puts it, "that began to break the vanilla." In May 1998, she graduated from the University of Colorado in Boulder with a major in international affairs and a minor in economics. Lindsay knew she was built for a leadership role in business; she began looking for a job that would prepare her for it. Companies that would put her through business school were at the top of her list. She chose the well-established Otis Elevator Company, founded in 1853.

"I was embarrassed to even say I worked at Otis," she says, smiling, "but I picked the job because they were recruiting really hard for young people as a dinosaur company with a lot of older people working there, and they paid so well, and they would send me away for training for three months and pay for business school. It was all about young professional development."

A month out of college, the twenty-one-year-old landed happily on the bottom step of the corporate escalator, selling for Otis in San Francisco. Lindsay was excited about the job and enjoyed the months of training. She lived with friends and was preparing for a marathon in the spring. But a marathon of another sort was about to begin.

A few weeks before Lindsay was scheduled to run the Big Sur marathon near Carmel, she felt a persistent irritation on the inside of her mouth, on the right side. She was mildly bothered by it but thought it would go away.

"I get cold sores on my lips, and so I thought it must just be some sort of canker sore near my back molar," she describes, "and when I spoke it was rubbing against my back molar, so it was annoying."

Lindsay made an appointment to see her primary care doctor, who looked at the inside of her mouth and told her it didn't look like anything troublesome. She advised her to see an ear, nose, and throat specialist if it didn't go away. A week later, the stubborn canker sore remained. Lindsay set up an appointment with an ENT, Dr. Daniel Hartman at the California Pacific Medical Center in San Francisco. He examined Lindsay, tweezed a sample from her mouth, and told her he would run a few tests. When he offered to give her medicine for the irritation, she declined, not wanting any meds in her body for the marathon. She was running the race on Sunday.

"He said, 'Okay, we'll run a few tests and we'll touch base on Monday.'"

Monday morning, Lindsay took a call at work from the doctor's office.

"The assistant called me and said, 'Hey, when you come to your appointment today, bring someone with you.'" Lindsay laughs. "Which is really a bad sign. But I'm twenty-two. I don't know this! And I said, 'Oh, why? Are you going to be giving me medication so I can't drive?' And she just said, 'No, no. We just thought you might not want to come alone.'" She laughs again. "I'm not going to call my mom—it's a canker sore!"

Lindsay showed up at the office alone.

"The doctor said, 'The test is positive.' And I went, 'Awesome!'" She chuckles at her naïveté. "And then he said, 'No, not awesome. You tested positive for squamous-cell carcinoma.' And I still didn't understand. I said, 'Okay, what do we do?' and he said, 'It's, um, cancer.'"

She was in shock. Dr. Hartman asked Lindsay if he could invite his partner, Dr. Nancy Snyderman, to join them. Confused and seated in a large, specialized chair—much like the one you sit in for an eye exam—Lindsay watched Nancy roll up to her on a stool.

"I remember her saying, 'It's okay. This is a kick in the pants. We'll get you through it, not a big deal. I'm here for you.'" Lindsay shrugs her shoulders. "She said it was going to be okay, so I believed her."

But Nancy knew it was not okay; the pairing of tongue cancer and a very young patient was sinister.

"It's very rare," Nancy explains, "and unfortunately it makes the prognosis really awful. I knew the odds, and the odds were against her."

The typical profile of a tongue cancer patient is an older man who's smoked and drunk for most of his life. Lindsay had no significant family history of cancer and was a healthy twenty-two-year-old. Nancy told Lindsay she'd just treated another young adult for tongue cancer. She was an attorney who did not want to lose the ability to speak, one of the risks of surgery for tongue cancer.

"She said, 'I've done this radical new approach. This is what we did. You don't have to worry. You're going to start radiation right away. We'll get the tumor, but you don't have to worry about any of this.' And I said to her 'Okay.' She was so confident and had a plan. Just what I needed."

Nancy had taken an approach that aligned perfectly with Lindsay's analytical, action-oriented mind.

Nancy sent Lindsay from the big chair to radiation to determine whether she was a candidate for the radical new approach she described. The staff told Lindsay that the person she brought with her to the appointment could come along.

Lindsay remembers, with a laugh, "I said, 'I didn't bring anyone for the canker sore.'"

Before she went to the radiation consultation, a stunned Lindsay dialed her mom.

"I called my mom at least nine times. Cell phones were kind of new then; she wasn't hip to the new technology. No answer. So I went through the entire radiation appointment alone," she says. "Someone else came in and said they needed to take a picture for my file. I'd been crying, I was so tense, and they said, 'Cheese.' It was the worst. I didn't remember a thing anyone there was saying to me."

After the appointment, she finally reached her mom.

"She answers and launches into, 'I'm at the Gap and can you believe I have been trying things on forever,' and on and on," Lindsay says, "'and I can't find my size . . . and oh, are you crying?' I said, 'Uh, I have cancer.'" She laughs. "At that point I was so annoyed that I really just said it like that."

She hung up with her stunned mother and called her dad.

"I hadn't spoken to him in a month," she says. "He didn't even know I had a canker sore, let alone cancer. He said, 'Excuse me? Who is this and what are you talking about?!'"

Lindsay left the doctor's office and entered Bizarro World. When she got home, Bob and her mom told her to get back in the car and drive the hour to their house. They did not want her to be alone in the city in her apartment.

"I remember driving home mad," she describes. "You know, music loud, angry. I remember walking into the house and seeing my mom and Bob and being like, 'Hi.' It felt so weird. I felt like, *I saw you yesterday at the marathon and we were celebrating my healthiest, happiest accomplishment, and then today everything's different, but I look the same, I feel the same.* But somehow everything had changed. We all sat there wondering, *What do we do now?*"

Drowning in the unknown, Lindsay knew an action plan would serve as her life preserver. She booked her MRI, checked into her Otis health benefits, and heeded a warning from Nancy: stay off the Internet.

"She said, 'Every test that's ever been done on this cancer is on eighty-year-old men who have smoked their whole lives. There is no study on a twenty-two-year-old girl who ran a marathon yesterday. So do not do it. You're going to look and it's going to scare you, and it doesn't apply to you.'"

Nancy felt protective of Lindsay, a very young, very sick girl who was now her patient.

"Adorable, charming, scared to death. She was like a doe caught in the headlights—not even a deer. She was petrified to the point that even at the very beginning, I said to her mom, 'I want you to bring in a tape recorder or a pen and paper and write things down because Lindsay isn't gonna be able to hear anything.' When you're shocked with a cancer diagnosis, you think you hear and that you're listening, but the reality is, you can't absorb it."

Nancy offered Lindsay her cell phone number and told her to call her every night and ask her anything.

"I knew that the questions with her would come incrementally," says Nancy, "and I wouldn't be able to give her everything in one session, and I wanted her to have access to me at any time."

Lindsay rarely talks about Nancy without a smile on her face. She loves and admires her doctor, who is now a dear friend. (Nancy also serves as NBC's chief medical editor.) Lindsay shared with me several of what she calls "Nancy-isms" throughout our conversations, and they are personal approaches and philosophies she holds dear. (I'll share them with you, too, in a while.) From a doctor-patient standpoint, the pair worked well together from the start.

"If you ask her now," says Lindsay, "she'll say, 'I don't know where Lindsay got all the hope. Her diagnosis was so aggressive.' But she, for me, played such a maternal role and gave me action steps, which of course I like. I just listened and did them. That made sense to me."

Lindsay says the days after the diagnosis are a blur. She told her roommates, who helped execute a phone tree to share the news with friends. Interestingly, the placement of Lindsay's cancer was not just horrifying, it made her feel vulnerable.

"I asked Nancy, 'Will I be able to kiss?' I was embarrassed, because I was afraid that if I was thinking about intimate things, people who heard I had tongue cancer would be thinking the same thing."

Traditional treatment for tongue cancer called for surgery first, then follow-up radiation and chemotherapy if needed. But Nancy's approach was to tackle it in reverse: shrink the tumor with radiation first so the need to surgically remove a large piece of the patient's tongue would be lessened. This struck a chord with Lindsay, because in all her other doctor interviews, the focus was solely on curing her, with no future vision about the quality of her life if she did survive. She wasn't an eighty-year-old man who might be willing to live with losing his ability to speak and writing on a dry-erase board for the remainder of his life. Nancy honored who Lindsay was. Their plan was to not only keep her alive, but to make sure she could talk and eat and kiss.

"She was an extraordinary partner from the very beginning," Nancy says. "It was Lindsay and me in partnership, and it made my job easier and harder."

Following an MRI, Lindsay was to immediately start eight weeks of radiation on the right side of her tongue. She describes the daily treatments as a nightmare.

"Every day I got locked to the table by my head," she says, clutching her head. "You get this crazy mask and it locks you in so you can't move."

I hear my first story of one of her "Lindsay Moments," as she refers to them. She will be the first to tell you, she is not someone who likes to be told no.

"Imagine this," she says. "They fitted my mask and they're testing it, so I'm locked to the table. It's very *Silence of the Lambs,* and I have one little straw to breathe out of. They say, 'The tattoo people are coming in now and they're going to tattoo you with the lasers on you so they get you all lined up.'"

Standard procedure is to permanently mark patients so that each time they come in, the radiation therapist can quickly and precisely pinpoint the area that needs treatment.

Laughing, she says, "I begin flailing!" She swings both arms in the air back and forth. "'Noooo! You're not!' One, I'm afraid of needles, and two, I've always said I'll never get a tattoo. It's just not my thing. I am flipping out and hell-bent on stopping this."

The therapists told Lindsay this was what was done; there were no options. (There's that word.)

"So I say, 'Can you use permanent markers?' They come back with, 'You'd have to touch it up every day and it has to be very accurate.' I tell them I'll touch it up. I'm thinking, *I am getting married one day. I am going to wear a wedding dress and I'm not having tattoos right here.*" She runs her hand across her upper chest area. "No way."

They say they have to call Nancy.

"So, guess what? Permanent markers."

And so began the alliance between Lindsay and Nancy, both dead set on life and quality of life.

"I let her be in the driver's seat as much as possible," Nancy says, "because when patients are sick, they never feel like they're in the driver's seat."

The eight weeks of radiation Lindsay underwent included a two-pronged attack. It would prove to be so draining that Lindsay had to move home so her mom could drive her to appointments and help her recover. Every day for six weeks she was given standard radiation. The final two weeks required a special hit that was especially horrific.

"They'd put me to sleep every day for two weeks. They'd pull my tongue out of my head, all the way out, so it was like . . ." She grabs her tongue and yanks it out. "My tongue was pierced with a thing on it so they could pull it out and hook it to a board, and then they would radiate just where the tumor was."

Lindsay worked at Otis during the first four weeks of radiation treatments, but exhaustion and pain drove her to take partially paid medical leave. She was supposed to be having the time of her life— starting a career, building her future—but instead, Lindsay was battling to survive. Looking back, she forgives herself for some of her young flights of fancy that served as pressure valves.

"I came in one day for treatment and said, 'I'm going to Vegas.'" She chuckles. "'My college friends are having a reunion. We graduated a year ago and we're all meeting in Vegas, and we're staying at the Venetian for the weekend.'"

Another Lindsay Moment, another call to Nancy.

"She sat me down and she said, 'No sun, no smoking, no drinking because of the pain meds. But if you want to go, you can.'"

I ask Nancy why she let her go.

"She had a life to live, and I was always weighing the fact that, frankly, I knew that what we were trying to accomplish was nearly impossible. I thought her life could be short, and what the hell; life is full of experiences, and I knew that she would remember that as a wonderful time, and the downside was minimal," she explains. "I knew that because I had earned her trust, that if I gave her ground rules, she would honor them."

Lindsay did go, sat in the shade, shopped, and enjoyed several spa treatments. Again, she was grateful to Nancy for artfully managing both her disease and her personality.

"She from the start looked at me like, 'You're not tongue cancer, you're Lindsay.'"

Even after Lindsay completed her eight weeks of radiation treatments, the side effects stuck around. The radiation continues to damage tumor cells for several weeks following the end of scheduled treatments. Lindsay's neck and tongue were raw, it hurt to speak and eat, and she slowly lost her sense of taste. There was a risk she would never regain it. Her sour, bitter, and salty components disappeared first.

"The last to go for me was sweet," she says. "I remember running through the house looking for licorice and then tasting it, realizing, *I could taste it yesterday and now it's gone*. I also remember walking into the house and it smelling so good, but then sitting down to eat and, nothing. It was really, really hard."

Four months after her radiation, still no taste. She began to adjust by "tasting" the mouth-feel of food.

"You start to crave things by texture. I would say, 'I really want something warm and creamy,' or 'I want something crunchy.'"

Lindsay's taste buds eventually responded, but not at full strength.

"Even now, when I eat blue cheese or garlic, I want more of it than most people would prefer," she explains, "because I don't taste it as intensely."

By August 1999, Lindsay had completed radiation and was ready to get back to work. But not necessarily at Otis. As grateful as she was for the company's solid health care benefits and paid medical leave, Lindsay began reevaluating her career and her life. She referred to her monthly medical checkups as mental health visits because they provided both relief and hope. Lindsay moved out of her mom and Bob's house and into an apartment. She decided to sample the dynamic and hip dot-com industry.

"I started by temping because I wasn't sure what I wanted to do," she says, "and I also heard that was a secret strategy to get a job at a dot-com. If they weren't hiring but you got in and you were good, they kept you. I also didn't know if I could physically work all day. Could I actually sit at a desk for forty hours?"

Lindsay temped at a dot-com company called Gazoontite that sold allergy and asthma products online, through a catalog, and in retail stores. She was one of the early hires at the company. Her temp job was to mail out the FedEx packages from the front desk and to sit in on fund-raising meetings to make the company look larger. The woman who headed up business development saw that Lindsay was bright and offered her a job after a month. But by the next year, many of the grossly overvalued dot-coms became known as the dot-bombs; tech stocks crashed, the bubble burst, and the cash-poor companies, including Gazoontite, filed for bankruptcy in the fall of 2000. In a whirlwind year, Lindsay gained valuable business experience and a mentor in the woman who hired her.

"She was such a great, dynamic businesswoman, someone I admired and looked up to; I learned so much from her," she explains. "We raised a ton of money and then a year later went bankrupt, like all the dot-coms. But, in that time, we created a medical advisory board, we had to penetrate the allergy and asthma market, and I got introduced to a business plan. We went to medical conferences, and I listened in on meetings where they were trying to raise money."

Lindsay's world for a solid year had been work. So fast was the pace in the dot-com industry, the office became dot-commers' social outlet, too, as they ate, slept, and breathed the Internet mania. When Gazoontite closed, Lindsay finally came up for air. She quickly realized that for her, San Francisco harbored bad memories.

"Everything reminded me of being sick," she says. "Every hospital, every street. And more importantly, I'm now twenty-four, and I'd go out with my friends, and guess what happens? 'This is my friend Lindsay, the one who had cancer, remember?' I just couldn't get away from it, and as a single girl in a small social group, I knew I would never meet Prince Charming there, because everyone was scared away."

A severance package allowed Lindsay to explore her next move. She decided to visit friends in New York City. Instantly, she fell in love with the anonymity the Big Apple provided: clean slate, no reminders. She said good-bye to her parents and moved to New York in October.

"They were really shocked," she says with a laugh. "I think my mom was solely supportive on the Prince Charming basis. As in, 'You're not going to meet a boy in San Francisco. If you're going to fall in love, you need to get out of here.' And that alone sold my mom."

In New York, Lindsay began interviewing for jobs in business development and the tech world. She was hired in November by a company called Jupiter Research that tracked the success and failure of dot-coms. Her new job and a mental reboot would begin in a week. Lindsay was happy and hopeful. Until her fingertips detected trouble.

"I used to have a habit of rubbing my neck when I was nervous, like this," she says, using one hand to touch both sides of her neck, "and there was a lump right here that was bothering me."

The pea-sized lump was on the right side of her neck. Nancy referred her to a doctor in the Bronx for a needle biopsy. Several days later, Lindsay was shopping with friends at J.Crew in Rockefeller Center when her phone rang. The doctor asked her to come in and talk about the results of her biopsy.

"But I said, 'Just tell me.' And he said, 'I'm not telling you over the phone. Where are you? Who are you with?' And I was thinking, *Okay, this is bad news. I'm schooled in this now,*" she says with a smile. "So, I got the news standing right there, in November, in front of the Christmas tree in Rockefeller Center with my friends. And then I had to call my job and say, 'I can't start Monday.'"

I ask Lindsay what it's like to hear that you have cancer for a second time.

"I remember that moment I felt numb. I felt like I was expected to cry or be upset, but really I felt shock and I was mad. My anger kicked in. The second time around in some ways is a lot harder, and in other ways a lot easier. Easier in that I felt like, *Okay, I'll go in tomorrow; we'll knock out our plan.* I knew the routine and the vernacular. But it was scarier in that the stakes were higher." She pauses. "The survival rates aren't as good if it comes back, and I wasn't convinced I'd be able to keep my tongue. I never thought I would die the first time around, but the second time around, I wasn't so sure. And I wasn't so sure that if I survived, the quality of life would be one that I wanted."

Lindsay's new apartment, new job, and fresh start would have to take a backseat to surgery. She moved back in with her mom and Bob in the San Francisco Bay Area.

"This option was an incredible luxury," Lindsay says. "I was so grateful for their endless emotional and financial support."

They agreed to pay several months' rent on her New York apartment, knowing it was a light at the end of this all-too-familiar tunnel for Lindsay.

"This is November, so I thought, *I'll go home, have surgery, and be back after the holidays. See you after Christmas! Everyone have a great break!*" She laughs, looking back. "That was the plan."

The search for surgeons began. Lindsay met with Nancy, who told her how she would approach the surgery. Her plan was to remove as little of Lindsay's tongue as possible depending on what she found. Nancy would then either sew Lindsay up or add a skin graft from her buttocks to give the tongue more meat. Her mission was two-fold: remove the cancer and preserve Lindsay's quality of life. They scheduled a surgery date. But, because the stakes were so high, Lindsay wanted a second opinion. Nancy not only supported the decision, she got Lindsay an appointment at the renowned MD Anderson Cancer Center in Texas. Lindsay and her mom flew to the appointment and entered the big leagues of cancer.

"My mom was always by my side, especially when making tough decisions like these. She was my pillar of strength and had to put up with a lot," Lindsay says. "I'm a lot to handle on a good day, let alone trying to deal with cancer. My mom was my everything. She was my advocate, my friend, my caregiver, my chauffeur, my shoulder to cry on, my coach, my chef, my strength."

Nervous and scared, Lindsay says she was not prepared for the realities of the head-and-neck-cancer ward at MD Anderson.

"I walked around the corner," she remembers, "and saw the waiting room and a patient walking toward me missing half his face. I screamed out loud. Sitting in that waiting room will haunt me forever."

Her visit with the highly respected surgeon went about as well. He told Lindsay he would aggressively tackle the cancer by removing two thirds of her tongue. He would then add a skin graft using part of her leg or arm. He would also incorporate veins and muscle so she would have blood flow in what remained of her tongue. She would need to stay at MD Anderson for weeks.

"They tell me all of this and I am beside myself. I don't want to do it," she says. "I'll never be able to speak again. I'm going to have this crazy tongue. This option felt like Frankenstein. When I heard this new option I felt like, *What else don't I know? What am I not asking? Should I not even consider the small center where they didn't even tell me about this?* So I leave and call Nancy. She's in her car in the parking garage, and I say, 'Why didn't you tell me about this?!' I am mad, and I don't want to do this."

Nancy let Lindsay release all her fear and anger.

"I remember saying, 'Lindsay, come home. I didn't cancel your OR time.' For some reason I didn't cancel it, and I didn't tell anybody. And y'know, OR time is a hot commodity and people could use the time. But, I don't know," she says, "something just told me to save it."

Part of the reason Lindsay felt so frustrated was that doctors had confirmed she had cancer in her neck, but they couldn't confirm that the spot they saw on her tongue was cancer or precancer. Her world felt out of control. She thought long and hard about whether to trust a small private practice or rely on the experience of a major cancer center. In the end, it had nothing to do with buildings. Lindsay went with the person who was, once again, focusing not just on saving her life but preserving the quality of her life if she survived.

"Nancy said, 'I am going to go in there and decide what to do once I know what's there.' The other doctor said, 'This is what I'm going to do regardless of what's there.'"

The week after Thanksgiving, Lindsay was admitted to the California Pacific Medical Center. She was very nervous in the operating room, wondering whether she'd be able to talk again after the surgery. Nancy and Dr. Hartman were in the room and a nurse put in her IV. The next thing Lindsay knew, Nancy was talking in her ear.

"Do you like how you sound? Talk."

So, Lindsay talked.

"I'm talking and I'm getting mad," she says, "I'm thinking, *Of course I like how I sound. Get this over with!*"

Nancy continues. "I need you to sing the ABCs. Start singing."

Lindsay went through the ABCs and also recited nursery rhymes at Nancy's request.

"Sally sells seashells . . ."

Nancy and Dr. Hartman kept Lindsay talking.

"We did 'seashells by the seashore,' then we did 'dee dee dee, ba ba ba.' Every little tongue twister my partner and I could think of from our childhood we had Lindsay do." Nancy adds with a chuckle, "And she did them groggy."

A groggy and confused Lindsay just wanted Nancy to start the surgery. When she woke up in the recovery room, she was convinced she couldn't talk. She was aggravated by the nurses who were asking questions, knowing she couldn't speak.

"In comes this woman in a ball gown," Lindsay says. "It's Nancy and she's on her way to a black-tie event. She starts talking to me, and I'm looking at her like, *I can't talk!* I've even convinced myself that they had to do the skin graft because I can feel that my butt hurts where they took skin. At this point, my tongue is very swollen, too."

An angry Lindsay sees Nancy lean in to her.

"She said in my ear, 'Right now you're swollen, and it's going to sound funny, and it's going to hurt, but do you remember doing the nursery rhymes? Can you hear yourself? That was *after* surgery. That is what you'll sound like when you're not swollen anymore. Hold on to that.'"

Lindsay calls that a golden moment.

"I was like the Cheshire cat!" she says with a huge smile. "I just started nodding and crying."

The frustrating she-sells-seashells moments that Lindsay recalls were actually Nancy deciding whether to add the skin graft to Lindsay's tongue.

"I had this beautiful young woman who entrusted her speech, and her swallowing, and the movement of her face to me, so I wanted to make sure that I didn't have her tongue tethered too much, because if I did, I had a couple of other tricks up my sleeve," Nancy says, "so I woke her up."

Lindsay says, amazed, "She woke me up in the middle of surgery. She stitched my tongue loosely and woke me up. She had the anesthesiologist bring me back and she had me sing. That's when she said, 'Do you like how you sound? If you like how you sound I'm just going to stitch you up.' There's a risk with the skin graft that if you put too much skin on you'll sound thick tongued, so she didn't want to cross that line."

Lindsay's surgery also included the removal of lymph nodes from her neck, where the cancer had spread. Approximately forty were taken out to be safe and would be tested for cancer. About a third of Lindsay's tongue was removed, a wedge from the inside layer. She's able to speak well today because the surface area of her tongue is not compromised; her tongue is simply thinner, which only slightly affects its mobility.

In Lindsay's ideal world, she'd have returned to her New York City apartment after the holidays and begun her new job at Jupiter. But a lab report put a perilous snag in those plans. It indicated that a toxic node may have released some of its cancer into Lindsay's system. The ante was upped; both radiation and chemotherapy were now in play. A newfangled technique had been developed that might allow Lindsay to tolerate a second round of radiation. She was devastated, now familiar with the rigors of treatment.

"I remember saying to my mom, 'Nancy called and said I'm a candidate for radiation,' and I said to my mom, 'I will not do it. It's too hard.' So we went the next day to talk to the doctor about radiation," she says. "And when they told me the statistics, I was in. What are you going to do? Do you want a ten percent chance of survival or fifty percent?"

It was the end of November 2000, and 2001 was looking bleak. Once the calendar page turned, Lindsay would undergo radiation treatments on her neck every morning and every night for a month. She would have overlapping chemotherapy treatments once every three weeks for three months. But until she healed from surgery, no one could touch her. She had eight weeks now to recuperate and to develop an action plan.

"That's when I started having doctors' appointments to learn what was next. What are my options, what are the side effects? What do the next few months look like?"

At twenty-four, Lindsay was now in the second fight for her life. Her hopes and dreams were eclipsed by a daily existence of healing and gearing up for the next battle.

"My day was spent high on pain meds, lying in bed, watching *ER* and movies. I felt like an old person, where a big day was going to see a doctor," she says, laughing. "And that takes all of your energy. You have to get dressed, go, come home, and you're wiped."

Lindsay met with an oncologist to discuss the chemo treatments that would begin in February. She was armed with a notebook full of questions and listened as he outlined the litany of side effects. She had written down *Fertility?* but never brought it up since the doctor didn't include it in the list of potential side effects. She left the appointment but was bothered by her assumption that infertility was not a concern. Lindsay made a follow-up call to the doctor.

"And that's when he said something to the effect of, 'Yes, there's up to a ninety percent chance you'll be infertile.' I remember hanging up, crying, and not knowing what to do. I thought, *I'm not doing it. I'm not doing chemo.*"

Unless a patient's testicles or ovaries are irradiated—which Lindsay's ovaries were not—radiation does not affect fertility. But chemotherapy is systemic, affecting the entire body, including reproductive organs. This was unacceptable to Lindsay. She'd always dreamed of having a family.

"We have pictures of me when I was little with a balloon or a pillow in my belly under my shirt," she says, "and when different aunts or uncles or cousins were pregnant I was the nurturing one."

There was that other component, too, that fueled Lindsay's indignation: Don't tell her no.

"When fertility was like that for me, a no, I was like, *No, no, no.* I did not like the idea that they were saying no to me on something so important. I also felt, and still do, so annoyed by this focus on temporary side effects. *Why are we talking about hair loss, nausea, vomiting, and smoking medical pot? I don't care about any of that. It's all temporary and I'll get through it. But infertility is permanent.* The goal was to cure me and to have a normal life, and fertility was part of that for me."

Lindsay told Nancy she would not expose her body to chemotherapy.

Nancy was blunt. "She told me she wanted to get pregnant, and one of the first things I said to her was, 'Lindsay, I don't care if you ever get pregnant. My job is to save your life. My job is to take care of you.' Lindsay looked at me and said, 'It's not *my* goal.' And there was this moment where I realized I was the doctor and she was the patient and we had very, very, very different goals in mind," says Nancy.

"I said to her, 'Your pregnancy is the least of my concerns. I want you around so you can even think about being pregnant.'"

This was one "no" to which Lindsay had to say yes.

"Nancy gave me the 'This isn't a choice' discussion, which was really the first time I felt like I wasn't in control," she says, laughing. "I thought, *I'm making the calls here!* and really I wasn't. They were making the calls and leading me to believe I was in control. But that's when she said, quite poignantly, 'I want you alive in five years so you can consider having a family. None of this matters if you're dead. You need to do this.'"

Lindsay agreed but began to explore a solution. During these recovery days on the couch, a particular movie she watched included a line that stuck with her. In *You've Got Mail,* the Tom Hanks character has a father who marries multiple times. One of his wives is a woman in her twenties.

"And Tom Hanks says to her, 'Where are you off to today?' and she says, 'Oh, I'm harvesting my eggs,'" Lindsay recalls, "and this was planted in my head. So, I asked my oncologist, 'Can I do this? Can I freeze my eggs?' He was not opposed to it, but his knowledge of fertility treatments was limited. He said, 'It takes six months to do those things, and you have six weeks before we have to start treatment.'"

Lindsay took it upon herself to quickly hunt down her options. She didn't have access to medical libraries and wasn't familiar with the Internet sites that allowed visitors to research links to medical journals, articles, and databases. The phone was her research tool of choice. It still hurt to speak, but she repeatedly called major reproductive centers around the country.

"I learned a lot in the process, because when you call you're getting a receptionist, and different receptionists answer at different times and they all tell you something different. One receptionist told me, 'They're only doing egg freezing on sheep in Virginia and it's not available for humans.'" She laughs. "But I'm thinking, *I saw it in the movie!*"

Lindsay was not getting anywhere, until one day when serendipity got her everywhere.

"On my fourth or fifth call to Stanford Fertility and Reproductive [Medicine] Center, someone picked up the phone by mistake. It was five o'clock and she picked up the wrong line and got me," she says, smiling. "And when I told her my story she said, 'Oh. We have a brand-new egg-freezing protocol for cancer patients that just launched.' And literally, I went the next day."

Hope finally eclipsed despair. She met with Dr. Lynn Westphal, who approved her as a candidate for the new protocol. Lindsay was game for anything she had to do to preserve her fertility before starting chemo.

"At that point I felt like I had already turned over my body and my life to medicine. My days were filled with doctors' appointments. I was already being poked and prodded every day. So the idea that I got to go to a doctor's appointment that I wanted to go to was hopeful. I was actively planning for my future; all of that was so wonderful."

But January 2001 would reveal both wonderful and awful news. Lindsay's best friend from preschool who became her sister, Kristi, was in a fight for her own life. Born with cystic fibrosis, Kristi developed an infection in December and was hospitalized. By January, her body was so resistant to antibiotics that the infection took over. Kristi and Lindsay were at the same hospital, Kristi in ICU, Lindsay going twice a day to the radiation lab. Tragically, Kristi died on January 7. One of the darkest days of Lindsay's life included radiation in the morning and Kristi's funeral in the afternoon, followed by a treatment to freeze her eggs. Her mom and Bob were beyond devastated.

"I was going to get cancer treatments and they were going to look at caskets," she says. "It was a very hard time."

Because her mom and Bob were dealing with Kristi's death, Lindsay was on her own during her fertility battle. On her first day in the Stanford IVF clinic, Lindsay realized she was not the typical patient.

"This man said to me, 'Are you an egg donor?' and I responded indignantly, 'I have cancer, mister.' His wife told him, 'You. Don't talk again.' She was mortified." Lindsay laughs. "But you can just imagine, here I am, twenty-four, sitting in that reproductive clinic. Single."

Lindsay's insurance didn't cover the procedure, so the clinic got her donated drugs and offered the treatment at cost, which she asked her parents to fund. For the clinic, Lindsay was only the second newly diagnosed cancer patient to freeze her eggs. Knowing her deadline, the staff fast-tracked Lindsay on learning the protocol for IVF treatments.

"You normally go in and hear PowerPoint presentations. You learn how to use needles. Back then you had to mix the medications at home, and so they took me that morning, and what a normal IVF patient has weeks to learn, they taught me quickly."

Here's what Lindsay was trying to do in eleven days: Use medication to stimulate her body to produce eggs. Those eggs would be surgically removed and then frozen. Here's where she's unique. The typical IVF patient would not freeze the eggs, but instead fertilize them with sperm in the lab. The resulting embryos would then be implanted back into the patient's womb and ideally make a baby. But Lindsay was not yet there in her life. She was not ready to have a baby. While using a sperm donor and freezing her embryos instead of eggs would make for a sturdier unit (an egg has a higher water content than an embryo, and therefore is more vulnerable to breakage or DNA damage when frozen), Lindsay could not get on board with the idea of donor sperm. Her future husband's sperm would be ideal.

"Twenty-four, single, in the midst of hell; that was one thing too much. I couldn't add that on. I thought, *I'm going to freeze my eggs and*

I believe in technology. So you guys keep working on the science so that when I need them in a few years, you'll be more advanced. And I thought, *Either I'll do this and one day be able to use my partner's sperm or down the road we'll adopt.* I just didn't feel comfortable interjecting a third party at that point."

In order for Lindsay's body to be stimulated by the meds, she needed a daily shot in the backside. Depending on whether she was at home or staying at a friend's empty apartment in the city, Lindsay needed help.

"I was often home alone at night or with my girlfriends. So I was thinking, *Who can I see tonight that can give me a shot?*" She laughs thinking back.

"Bob gave me the shots some nights, and there were even nights when girlfriends did. One of my friends was in physical therapy school so she practiced her first shot on me." She chuckles. "I remember I was with another friend and she couldn't stomach it, so her boyfriend gave me the shot. Ha!"

In early February, it was time for radiation. Lindsay's insides were in for a wild ride.

"I would go to radiation in the morning, then I'd go to IVF clinic for blood work and ultrasound, then in the afternoon I'd go back to radiation, and then at night, I'd have the shots."

Lindsay's friends were supportive but felt afraid and skittish about the topic of cancer, which was riddled with emotional land mines. Her fertility adventure was a much safer way to connect.

"It was hopeful," she explains, "because it was about me surviving, and because it was about boys, and weddings, and babies, and motherhood, and all of the things that all of us single girls in the city were dreaming about."

Because Lindsay wasn't trying to get pregnant through IVF, doctors could hyperstimulate her ovaries in an effort to harvest as many eggs as possible. While the typical IVF patient (usually in her mid-to-late thirties) grows ten eggs, young Lindsay grew twenty-nine. However, there was one snag. The hyperstimulation resulted in a bloated belly for Lindsay, just as her chemo was scheduled to start.

"So, I got in trouble. I had to call my chemo doctor and say, 'I froze my eggs, everything went well, but I have a little problem.'" She laughs sheepishly. "I think it was delayed by maybe three days, but it turned out fine. I just spent a few days on the couch waiting for the hyperstimulation to go away."

As her chemotherapy date approached, Lindsay decided to put up one more fortress in her war against infertility. Dr. Westphal told her she could undergo a newly explored procedure to put her into a temporary menopause-like state. That way her ovaries would be protected during chemo. If it worked, she'd never need her frozen eggs. If it didn't, her eggs would be there for her.

"I felt like at that point, *Sure, who cares! I've already been put through the wringer, so a shot a month in my butt? I'll have hot flashes for three months? Who cares?*"

Lindsay was spinning multiple medical plates: twice-daily radiation, chemotherapy once every three weeks, and a menopause-inducing Lupron shot once a month. Her journey was challenging, but it had a silver lining coated in ice: twenty-nine frozen eggs safely stored away.

"I was actively planning for my future," she says, "and on some level that made me believe I would live. I wanted to live now."

Lindsay's social interaction was largely with people in cancer support groups and who were undergoing chemo treatments in the Bay Area. During her appointments, she'd sit in a room full of patients, all receiving chemo and related drugs prepared in bags that hung on IV poles. They passed the six to eight hours by listening to music or talking.

"I remember I was euphoric from the egg-freezing experience," she says, "so I was talking to the nurses and the patients sitting next to me, and I quickly learned that this was not a good place to talk about this. I realized, *No one knows. I am essentially telling them they are being sterilized right then.* They did not know it. I remember this guy in the room, and he was asking me questions like, 'What do you mean? This is sterilizing me right now? I could have banked my sperm?' I remember him turning to the nurse and saying, 'Are you telling me that this thing in my arm right now is sterilizing me?'"

A breast cancer patient who was receiving chemo every week for fifty-two weeks was also stunned by what Lindsay was sharing.

"She was already a mom and wasn't interested in more kids, but said, 'I can't believe they didn't tell me. Did they assume that I was done having children?'"

Lindsay finished all her treatments in April 2001. The five-month medical marathon was over. A week later, she moved back to her apartment in New York City. Her parents were concerned that she'd feel alone, but Lindsay had gotten through the tunnel and now needed the light.

"Really, after being in their home through surgery and healing, then my sister's death and all my radiation and chemo, and everything in that house and bedroom, I thought, *I don't want to stay here for another minute.*"

Lindsay had received a severance check from Jupiter Research while she was still at home. The company had downsized, and her position—which she never filled—was eliminated.

She says with a smile, "Never one day on the job, and I got a huge check."

As spring moved into summer, Lindsay began to think. Ever since the realization that other cancer patients were not being in-formed about options to protect their fertility, she felt like she had a secret that needed to be shared.

"You get car insurance, but do you drive around hoping you get into an accident because you have it? No. It's the same with frozen eggs. You hope that you never have to use them, but if you do, you'll be really glad they're there."

She began researching whether it was standard practice to inform patients that infertility is a potential side effect of cancer treatment.

"I really felt in my head for a long time, *Am I making this up? Is it even an issue? Was I totally high on pain meds? Am I making a mountain out of a molehill?* I didn't fully trust myself on it yet."

The more Lindsay read and the more people she talked to, the more her concern was validated. She began to write a business plan for a foundation that would spread the word. When a friend found out what she was doing, he e-mailed her and encouraged her to meet a cancer survivor he'd seen speak at an event for the American Cancer Society. He told her the survivor, Doug Ulman, had started a foundation to support and educate young cancer survivors.

"I called him and said, 'Hey, I heard you started this nonprofit,'" she says. "'I have this inkling about a problem around fertility and I want to run it past you.'"

Coincidentally, she had called Doug during his first week as director of survivorship at the Lance Armstrong Foundation. He told her no one was addressing the issue, and that Lance and his wife Kristin would be interested in talking with her.

"It was interesting because at the time, Kristin was my hero," she says. "Lance has a good story, but Kristin answered all my hopes and fears. In an article I read, I learned that she met and chose Lance after his cancer. She talked a lot about how many of her friends thought she was crazy, like, 'Why are you falling in love with this man who almost died?' And she said, 'I'd rather have one year of wonderful than a lifetime of mediocre.' And I thought, *Oh, my gosh. It's possible for someone to love me. There may be a boy version of Kristin out there who will take the risk.*"

Lindsay continued to write her business plan and planned to have Kristin write the foreword. Her former mentor at Gazoontite helped

Lindsay structure the business plan, and Lindsay marveled at how her own brief work experience was paying off.

"So, what happens? When I go to write my own business plan, I know how. I've seen a medical advisory board being formed. I've gone to medical conferences. I know how to raise money. Every skill I learned enabled me to start the foundation."

As she honed her business plan, Lindsay ruminated on different names for the foundation and implemented Internet searches for already-taken trademarks. She ran her ideas by friends and narrowed down her choices to two: Fertile Hope or Fertile Options.

"I really liked Fertile Hope, but it bothered me a little bit. I kept thinking, *This is not just hope, these options are real. These are tangible scientifically proved options.* So I was really leaning toward Fertile Options because of that."

In a walk through Central Park, Lindsay listened to her girlfriend's argument that Fertile Options seemed boring, not warm enough for fund-raising, and not as effective from a design standpoint. Lindsay bought in.

"I was pressured away from what I wanted, to what everyone else wanted." She smiles. "And I'm so thankful. In the end it was such a better name."

As Lindsay continued to work and transition back into a treatment-free life, she experienced what many cancer survivors do: the feeling that you don't quite fit in.

"When I got back to New York, I felt that way. I didn't fit in because my friends were working all day and I didn't have a job, and then every night we're going out to dinner and, guess what? Everyone's smoking. This was all before the smoking bans were put in place in the city. All of these young kids are drinking and smoking and there's some drugs going on, and I'm thinking, *You all have healthy bodies and you're deliberately poisoning yourselves.* I was really struggling."

She jumped at the chance to nanny for a family who'd be spending the summer in Nantucket. The five children were all under the age of twelve.

"The real reason I wanted to go was that the mom is a venture capitalist, and I thought"—she says with a grin—"*I am writing a business plan and she can help me.*"

Lindsay enjoyed her summer in the secure bubble of an active family along with a healthy outdoor lifestyle. She returned to New York and completed her business plan in September. Her friends in the magazine industry had procured an article in *Allure* about her and Fertile Hope. On September 11, Lindsay was getting her makeup done for a photo shoot in a friend's apartment in the West Village when news broke on the television that a plane had hit one of the World Trade Center towers.

"And so we go up on the fire escape to see what happened to the plane, and a second plane goes in. We saw it live."

The 9/11 terrorist attacks unfolded in person for people in the city, and on live broadcasts around the world. Lindsay's parents encouraged her to come home, but she did so only for a visit. She felt the need to heal with her fellow New Yorkers who'd shared the horrors firsthand. Her plan to launch Fertile Hope in October was met with some skepticism.

"People were saying to me, 'You cannot start a nonprofit in New York City and compete with 9/11,'" she says. "'There will be no money coming your way.'"

But Lindsay was resolute. She was confident in her plan and her ability to execute it. Her dad generously offered to donate enough money to pay her a modest salary for a year until she got things up and running.

"Without seed money from my dad, I wouldn't have been able to give Fertile Hope my all," Lindsay says. "I felt spoiled by his gift and vowed to pay it forward."

Her financing was in order, but what of Lindsay's emotional state? As a brand-new cancer survivor, she considered whether immersing herself in cancer issues would be too stressful.

"People warned me about that," she says, "but I felt that at Fertile Hope I wouldn't be talking about cancer every day. There would be a very small amount that I'd need to know about someone's cancer to help them with fertility."

She was determined to proceed and was also encouraged about the quality of her life in New York. News began brewing that Mayor Michael Bloomberg was spearheading a sweeping ban on indoor smoking that would include nearly all bars and restaurants. With her business plan completed and a start-up grant from the family she worked for on Nantucket, Lindsay launched the Fertile Hope website in October. She'd read online about an annual meeting of the American Society for Reproductive Medicine slated for October in Orlando and decided to attend. Her goal was to determine whether she was on the right path and to ask some of the doctors to be on the foundation's medical advisory board.

"I had to go buy a suit. I had no 'big girl' clothes. I flew to the conference and when I got there I thought, *Whose idea was this?*" She laughs. "It's just me and my flyer and I have no 'MD' after my name. I'm just a patient and I think this is important. I walked straight to the bathroom and started crying."

Admittedly shy about networking, Lindsay was mortified.

"I have to walk up to strangers, start talking to them about this idea that is very personal, I have never fund-raised before, I've never talked to these doctors, and I am twenty-five. In retrospect, I was very young."

In tears, Lindsay continued to doubt her decision to attend. But as the conference progressed, she began to meet doctors who introduced her to other doctors once they heard her pitch. By the first evening, she had scored an invitation to a dinner with doctors from Cornell, which houses one of the top IVF centers in the world. She was led into a car with Cornell's Dr. Zev Rosenwaks, the grand poobah of IVF, who trained under the doctor who pioneered in vitro fertilization.

"I am in a black town car in the middle seat on the hump, and Dr. Rosenwaks is next to me, and I have no idea who he is, so I'm just talking to him. 'Hi, my name's Lindsay,' and he said, 'How old are you?' We talked for a bit more and then again, 'How old are you?' When I told him twenty-five he said, 'My children are your age.' I remember thinking, *Who cares? Is this really an issue?*" she says, laughing.

Lindsay dined with some of the greatest minds in the IVF world, along with the most highly acclaimed published authors on the subject, and the very people who developed techniques she might employ one day to have children. Still not realizing the respect Dr. Rosenwaks commanded, Lindsay plopped down in the seat next to him since it was empty.

"We talked the whole night. He agreed to join my medical advisory board, he agreed that this was so important, and he wanted to help; he said Cornell would give me a grant."

The doctor also told Lindsay he'd tell the influential pharmaceutical companies to talk to her.

"The next day I had all these leads with fertility pharmaceutical companies; I'm up in their suites that I didn't even know existed." She shakes her head in amazement. "So, at each step of the way, there was validation, validation, validation. And it took off from there."

Now that Lindsay had identified that there was a real problem in communicating fertility options to cancer patients, she set out to find out why it was happening. She located a study published in the *Journal of Clinical Oncology* that asked oncologists whether they brought up fertility-preservation options with their male cancer patients. A sister study also asked male cancer patients if their doctors offered the information. Although 91 percent of the oncology physicians who responded agreed that sperm banking should be offered as an option to all men at risk of infertility because of cancer treatment, only 10 percent of them said that they informed their patients. Lindsay was most interested in the reasons why oncologists failed to broach the topic. According to the study results, the factors that were most likely to influence oncologists not to offer the sperm-banking option included:

- The patient is HIV positive
- The patient has a very aggressive disease and needs rapid initiation of cancer treatment
- The patient has a poor prognosis for survival
- The patient is open about being gay
- The patient does not have health insurance
- The patient already has at least one child

The results both appalled and motivated Lindsay.

"When I read that study," she says, "that was when I decided, *I'm in. I'm so in, because this is atrocious.*"

While Lindsay agreed that curing cancer was the bull's-eye in terms of the need for time and money, she had trouble understanding why the concept of offering up fertility preservation as a concern to cancer patients was so foreign.

"Focus on the cure, but in the meantime, there are some low-hanging fruit," she reasons. "We can solve this problem."

Fueled by all that she was learning, Lindsay dismissed other peoples' suggestions to her to introduce Fertile Hope slowly.

"Everyone was saying, 'You should start small. You should test the market and do a pilot program.' And I thought, *No way! If I do this only in New York, someone in Texas is getting sterilized! Someone in Chicago is getting sterilized!* That was the biggest thing for me," she says. "Once I uncovered the depth and breadth of the problem, every day it bothered me that people were being sterilized and they didn't know it. Every day, right now, at every cancer center, they are being sterilized. And right down the hall is a sperm bank or a reproductive clinic, and they could be doing this, but they don't know."

Lindsay began to talk with oncologists. She was confident they were first and foremost concerned with saving their patients' lives, but she wanted to know what else might be keeping the topic of fertility outside of the doctors' examining rooms. It soon became clear that, because IVF was an emerging technology, many doctors had gone to medical school before it even existed. For doctors who weren't familiar with the specialty, opening that can of worms—or sperm—was a deterrent to the conversation.

"They don't want to get inundated with a million questions, it's going to be a time suck, and it's hard on the ego," she says. "They don't want to admit ignorance on something, especially on the first day when they're trying to build your trust and confidence, and they don't want to deliver a double blow. 'Oh, by the way, you have cancer and you might end up infertile.' And many have common misconceptions about the area, such as, 'He came in without shoes; he can't afford sperm banking,' and when you ask the average oncologist how much he thinks sperm banking costs, he'll say thousands of dollars and it only averages six hundred dollars."

She knew Fertile Hope would offer oncologists a fast and easy way to refer their patients once they informed them that chemo could make them sterile.

"I'm not asking you to be a reproductive expert, but just like you advised, 'Go get your MRI, go get your flu shot, go get your X-ray, go do all these things before you start chemo,' just add, 'Go talk to a reproductive doctor,' or 'Here's a clinic.' I'm not asking you to become an expert; I just need you to make a referral."

A key problem Lindsay identified early on was that the world of oncology and the world of fertility did not overlap. Not only did doctors in both fields never communicate, they didn't see a need for it. Lindsay was a living example of why there indeed was a need; Lindsay and the more than 140,000 newly diagnosed cancer patients each year ages zero to forty-five (still in their reproductive years) deserved to be informed about their fertility options. She went about the business of presenting Fertile Hope.

"I had a business plan, plus I had two other plans of attack. 'Here's the market, here are the five ways we will achieve it. We can't do it all at once so here's how we prioritize.' Yes, I had the patient story for when doctors said, 'Patients don't care about this'; I could refute them. And when reproductive doctors said, 'Egg freezing is not an option; it doesn't exist,' I could say, 'Actually, my eggs are frozen.' But the real success of Fertile Hope stemmed from applying sound business solutions to a real problem."

As with any compelling cause, there was a risk of relying too heavily on emotions to raise funds or to spread a message. Lindsay deliberately developed a measured tone to promote Fertile Hope.

"I don't have a 'PhD' or 'MD' after my name, so if I go too far in the heartstrings approach, I lose them. They'll think, *This is an irrational, emotional patient*, as opposed to a polished, professional, knowledgeable woman advocating for something she believes in. I do think there had to be some patient component or an unbiased third party involved, because if a reproductive doctor goes in to make the pitch, in Gucci loafers and a fancy outfit, and walks in to the oncologist and says, 'Hey, send your patients to me. I can help them,' it's too salesy. But when a patient advocate comes in and says, 'Patients want this. You guys need to start talking,' it's less of a sales pitch. At the end of the day it benefits the reproductive center, but it also benefits the patient."

While Lindsay's patient status added credibility, her age had the potential to diminish it. She was twenty-five, heading up a nonprofit organization, and asking for money and tremendous change in the medical world. Her youth turned out to be, in some areas, helpful.

"Like with Dr. Rosenwaks, I felt that he was more likely to talk to me because of my age. I reminded him of his children. 'Let me help you.' There's something about that generation, and that's great. 'You're young, you're ambitious, you're smart.' But it also meant for me that we had to be overprofessional. I had to be overprepared, überprofessional, and I was criticized a lot. 'This looks very for-profit,' or 'This looks very professional. How much money did Fertile Hope spend on it?' But I felt like I had to err on that side."

The Fertile Hope website looked so professional, Lindsay says people assumed Cornell gave the foundation hundreds of thousands of dollars, when in reality, the grant was around $4,000. She asked friends to write source code for the site and launched it for thousands, not *hundreds* of thousands, of dollars.

"It would hurt us sometimes, because people would say, 'Oh, do you have a staff of forty?' At our biggest we had six people. We didn't have a lot of money, but we were so polished and professional on the front side. We had to suit up with a strong medical advisory board and an incredible board of directors. We had to pile on credibility everywhere we could, and then my age and lack of advanced degrees would be less of an issue."

The year 2001 for Lindsay had been astounding. It began with a battle for her survival and was now ending with the cultivation of Fertile Hope. Lindsay had no idea she was in store for another milestone in just a month.

In January, Lindsay was invited to a friend's birthday party at a New York City bar. She was introduced to a guy named Jordan Beck, who was with a woman she assumed was Jordan's girlfriend. Lindsay was quite put off when Jordan started hitting on her.

"I thought, *You creep! Your girlfriend is here!* So, then he buys me a drink! And I take the drink and basically run away to the bathroom."

The bathroom was located downstairs in the bar, and as Lindsay made her way there, she accidentally made her mark on someone heading up the stairs.

"I spilled my drink on a guy, who happened to be Marky Mark. Mark Wahlberg! Ha!" She giggles. "It's so New York, right? So now, Mark Wahlberg has a Cosmo, a pink drink, all down his shirt. And he says, 'Don't worry, baby,' and he takes off his shirt! And then, off he took."

(Lindsay says the shirtless Mr. Wahlberg danced the night away at the bar.)

Jordan, who worked on Wall Street, e-mailed a mutual friend a few days later to ask if Lindsay was single. When he learned she was dating someone else, he asked the friend to let him know if that ever changed.

"Two weeks later," Jordan says, "I got an e-mail saying, *Hey, you might want to give her a call now.*"

The call cleared up the identity of Jordan's "date" for the birthday party. He was there with the girlfriend of his roommate, who was not a fan of large social gatherings. Jordan asked Lindsay to go out, but the date of the dinner fell on the night before she was scheduled to appear on *Good Morning America* with Nancy to discuss Fertile Hope. Hmm . . .

"I want to go out," Lindsay recalls, "but I have to go to bed early, so I don't want him to think I don't like him if I leave early. So I had to say, 'I have this big thing for work tomorrow morning.' What I didn't know was that my friends had already told him that I was going to be on. So, the next morning he's e-mailing me from the trading floor where there are TVs everywhere, and he's saying, 'We're all going to turn on the show.' And I haven't told him anything about my cancer, my fertility, Fertile Hope, nothing!"

A panicked Lindsay e-mailed him back, telling him she didn't think that was a good idea and that she had some things she'd like to discuss in person.

"So, Jordan wrote right back and said, 'I already know your story and I'm totally fine with it and I'd like to learn more about it all and watch.' At that moment, I was like, *He's the one.* It was my Kristin Armstrong moment. *He already knew and he still asked me out!*"

Lindsay appeared on the morning program and went for a drink with Jordan that night. She told him he could ask her anything.

"And he thought for a minute, and I was really expecting a doozy of a question, and he said, 'What was it like? What was the set of *Good Morning America* like?'" She laughs. "And I was like, *Okay, he knows the cancer piece of me but it doesn't define me.* I hadn't had that experience yet. It was so cool."

Jordan was intrigued by this unique girl from California.

"She was much different than any New York girl or any girl that I had met," he says. "Really smart, calm, easygoing. Just a nice, normal, intelligent, attractive girl."

The topic of children came up early in the relationship, by chance, during Lindsay's third date with Jordan.

"He invited me to a client dinner and we were seated boy-girl-boy-girl around a round table, and the girl next to Jordan was very chatty and flirty and asked him how many kids he wanted. I thought, *Whoa, girl, I haven't even asked that yet!* He said, 'Four or five.' And again, I thought, *You're the boy for me.*"

Both Lindsay's foundation and her relationship with Jordan were growing strong. She was very up-front with him that she didn't know whether she was fertile, but that if she wasn't, she had frozen her eggs and she was in touch with the best IVF doctors in the world if they ever needed to go that route.

"Jordan would always say things like, 'We'll cross that bridge when we get to it. I want you, and if we want kids we'll make it happen, but we don't need to worry about that today. We're not trying to have babies today.' For him it was like, 'Why in the world would that be a reason I wouldn't date you?'"

Jordan says he's not sure why, but he never thought twice about it. He thought only that she was the type of person he wanted to date.

"You could tell from the ambition that she had and the way she lived life," he explains. "And I could tell that very quickly. It was so opposite of any girl I'd ever met that probably—very far back in my brain; these were not conscious thoughts—it was attractive."

That summer, the nanny job was available again for the Nantucket family, so Lindsay took it and Jordan visited every weekend. She could work on Fertile Hope from there and enjoy a glimpse into family life with Jordan.

"It was almost like playing house. We thought, *Wow, we could do this! This is fun!* He's an only child, so it gave him an idea of what it would be like to have five kids. We got exposed to those things together in a way that we both liked and wanted."

Lindsay's life was fulfilling both personally and professionally. She was running the foundation by herself and enjoying the challenge. The 800 number listed on Fertile Hope's website and literature rang straight to her cell phone.

"Callers would say, 'I was just diagnosed. What do I do?' and I was like, 'Okay, where are you? This is what you do.' And again, they thought the organization was way bigger than it was. They had no idea they were calling my cell phone as I was cruising around New York."

At first, she handled between ten and twenty calls per week, mostly from outraged cancer patients who'd already been rendered sterile.

"And that for me was incredibly motivating because it was validating," she says. "I was still wondering, *Did I make this up? Does this really happen to people?* Most of the people I was talking to up front were survivors who were really angry, and that really for me validated the need and it fueled my fire."

Lindsay's business plan never included the arena of legal action. Fertile Hope's mission was to inform people of their options. Don't assume you're fertile or infertile—get tested. Explore donor eggs or donor sperm. Is there any leftover sperm in the testicles? Lindsay was still amazed that the risk of sterilization was not on the informed-consent forms signed by cancer patients.

"The patient is in the land of the unknown. You don't know what to ask. Of course, if you knew fertility was a risk you would ask. But the cancer doctors are in the cancer world; they know. The patient is thrown in and expected to sink or swim. What if you don't by happenstance ask the right question?" she asks. "That shouldn't be how you get critical information. And I think sterilizing someone is critical information."

In November 2002, Lindsay's friends helped her organize a large fund-raising event for Fertile Hope in New York City. Kristin Armstrong, who was on the foundation's board of directors, asked Lance to speak at the event. The people and the fund-raising dollars rolled in. Several cancer survivors who attended became Fertile Hope volunteers, eager to donate their time to fund-raising, graphic design, and marketing. Just a few months later, in January 2003, one of the volunteers became Fertile Hope's first employee. Lindsay was also able to rent shared office space and hook up a phone and a hotline. Reproductive centers were now offering to sponsor Fertile Hope events and pharmaceutical money was coming in. Doctors in the reproductive field were amazed.

"They wondered, 'Who is this girl? Last year she was at the medical conference with a flyer, and the next year Lance Armstrong is speaking to us about how important this is, and in the meantime she has been in the *New York Times* and the *New York Post* and the *Wall Street Journal.*' It was all happening fast."

Fertile Hope launched with five areas to advance: awareness, education, financial assistance, research, and support. Lindsay knew they could not achieve them all at once and that each one would lead to the next with fund-raising as fuel for the forward movement. She was speaking all over the country, but mostly to fertility doctors. The reproductive world took quickly to the idea of Fertile Hope: new patients, new money, and a way to advance the technology of egg freezing. But the cancer world was not as receptive, an issue she hadn't anticipated.

"Fertile Hope became the darling of the reproductive industry very quickly," she explains, "but the cancer industry was so hard to penetrate, it was shocking. And that was hard for me, and frustrating. We had to really think harder. Every pharmaceutical company in the world was trying to do the same thing: How do you change physician practice? How do you integrate what you want into their day-to-day checklist? And here little Fertile Hope was trying to do that. We ended up doing it in six years, which is faster than most people can, but I expected from my dot-com glory days that that would happen in six months or a year."

A breakthrough came in fall 2002 after Fertile Hope sent out fifty thousand brochures, one to every cancer doctor and nurse in the country. A follow-up focus group helped the foundation to gather feedback and measure the impact of the mailing. What was the most effective way to get oncologists to refer their patients to Fertile Hope? Lindsay listened in as the focus group leader spoke with an anonymous doctor over the phone. His response proved to be a game changer for the foundation.

"He said, 'I am busy and I am not going to go to a meeting about fertility. I go to meetings about how to best treat my patients and do my job, and even if I'm at a conference where fertility is being discussed, it would probably coincide with another class that's more important to my patient's survival, so I won't go to it. But I am interested and I want to do right by my patient and do think this is important, but bring the information to me. Don't make me find you.' The leader followed up with, 'How do we get to you?'"

The doctor explained that every major hospital in the country does something called grand rounds, most often on a weekly basis. Presenters are brought in, and the goal is to help doctors and other health care professionals stay current on evolving areas that may be outside of their core practice; the newest research and treatments. The doctor said, "If you can penetrate that, you're in."

Lindsay immediately developed a business model for physician education via grand rounds.

"Our goal for the first year was to do ten major cancer centers and ten community hospitals," she says. "We blew those numbers out of the water."

Then came another creative idea: a way to get the local fertility doctors into grand rounds.

"Let's say we had a talk in Connecticut. So, we're going to go to Yale and do grand rounds at the cancer center with all the oncologists. We would call the local reproductive doctor there at Yale and say, 'Hey, we're doing grand rounds. Do you want to come and do the presentation with us?' Uh, yeah. Of course you do. So they would come and we wouldn't even give them an honorarium. 'We're not paying for anything. You come. It's a huge opportunity for you that you wouldn't have without us.' We would give a one-hour presentation and then all the oncologists would have the information they needed, all because that one doctor in that one focus group said, 'Come to me.'"

Blending the two worlds of oncology and reproduction was finally happening. Lindsay says a particular grand rounds session exposed the disconnect that was right before the medical community's eyes.

"I'll never forget this. We were at the Cleveland Clinic doing grand rounds, and it was me and the female reproductive doctor and the male reproductive doctor. The male doctor gets up and says, 'Before we get started I just want to see a show of hands as to who knows where the Cleveland Clinic sperm bank is?' And no one raised a hand. And then he says, 'See out the window? There's a courtyard. It's right there. You can see it out the window. Just so you all know, it's right there.'"

Nancy puts herself in the category of cancer doctors who needed to look beyond their specialty.

"Do you think that I ever once thought about a woman's uterus or ovaries? I can tell you, until I met Lindsay, never. My ecosystem was the head and neck. I wanted her to speak, swallow, and breathe as normally as possible, and those are three things we do every day and take for granted, but if I don't fix you right, you're not going to do them. So my goal was—this beautiful voice, she loved to eat food, she loved red wine—to be able to return her to those things. Did I ever once think about her ovaries? No," she admits. "Now, I know this is going to sound callous, but did I care about her ovaries? No. My job was to cure her; to give her a life the best I could, and to save the things that were in my control. What she did was say to me, 'Hey, guess what, doc? Not good enough. I expect you to get me to swallow and speak and breathe again because that's your job. But in the meantime, you need to have a conversation with this doctor and this doctor and this doctor, because I don't understand the side effects of all the sort of stuff you've ordered for me.' And I was like, 'Really?' And guess what? I did. She taught me."

In October 2003, Jordan proposed to Lindsay. They were married eight months later. Nancy and Dr. Hartman went to the wedding. A photo Nancy treasures hangs on her office wall.

"There is a picture of the beautiful bride smiling, and he and I are on either side of her kissing her cheeks, and people come into my office and say, 'Oh! Is this you and your husband and your daughter?'" She laughs. "And I say, 'No, but it's my favorite picture of any wedding I've ever been to.' If they would have told me that I would see her walk down the aisle with this stunningly handsome man I would have never believed it."

Dr. Daniel Hartman, Lindsay, Dr. Nancy Snyderman, 2004.
(Credit: Michelle Walker Photography)

In the fall of 2004, Fertile Hope launched Sharing Hope, a financial assistance program for fertility preservation. The goal was to increase access to egg freezing, embryo freezing, and sperm banking for newly diagnosed cancer patients whose medical treatments put them at risk for infertility. Fertile Hope worked with companies and clinics to arrange for discounted services and donated medications for eligible female and male cancer patients. The newly married

Lindsay was also launching a personal mission: get pregnant. She had stopped taking birth control pills prior to the wedding and was a bit concerned because her cycle became very erratic. She developed severe cramps, pesky yeast infections, and long, heavy periods. Lindsay had the gut feeling that she was possibly having miscarriages. She made an appointment in October with Dr. Rosenwaks for herself and Jordan to see if they were both fertile. Tests indicated each was, and the doctor encouraged the pair to try to get pregnant on their own. By the next month, Lindsay was pregnant, but within a week, she miscarried. The stress was mounting for Lindsay. She was having problems staying pregnant, and due to her prior cancer treatments, the biological calendar of her ovaries was ten to fifteen years shorter.

"I really felt, in that moment, that infertility was harder than cancer ever was, because you're always in the land of the unknown. *I don't know why I'm miscarrying, I don't know why it's not working, I don't know, I don't know, I don't know.* With cancer you're always in action mode. There's a plan every day. *Today I killed my cancer. I had radiation.* That's very active. But with infertility, you can't do anything for weeks. You just have to sit around and wait. I found it very hard."

Plus, she was haunted by a conversation she'd had with a doctor prior to a speaking engagement at Yale. She had miscarried in her hotel room before giving a speech to oncologists. Sad and desperate for answers, Lindsay secretly presented her own case to the local reproductive doctor she appeared with at the presentation.

"I lied and said, 'This woman called me this morning and here's her case.' I laid out *my* case, and he said to me, 'There's no hope. She needs donor eggs. You need to call her and tell her it's not going to work.' So I asked him, 'What if it's on the male side?' And he said, 'That *never* happens. That's like a point-five percent possibility.'"

Lindsay had survived cancer, found her Prince Charming, preserved her eggs, and now she couldn't get pregnant. She was thankful she could help other people manage their fertility, but she felt aggravated that she had no control over her own.

"The challenge of running my own organization and having it overlap with my life," she admits, "happened with the fertility piece, not the cancer piece. I found it very hard to go to work every day. I couldn't get away. My life at home was all about fertility and my life at work was all about fertility, and that was very hard."

Lindsay wanted to explore every avenue of what could be causing the problem, so in early 2005, Dr. Rosenwaks ordered a karyotype test for both Lindsay and Jordan. It's basically a blood test to identify and evaluate the size, shape, and number of chromosomes in a sample of body cells. The test could determine whether a chromosome defect was preventing Lindsay from becoming pregnant or causing miscarriages. Lindsay was standing in Penn Station en route to a work conference when her phone rang. It was Dr. Rosenwaks.

"He said, 'Lindsay, I'm so sorry. We got the test results and we uncovered that Jordan has a rare genetic abnormality that's causing the miscarriages.' And he had his bad-news voice on, the voice he uses when he says, 'I'm sorry, you've miscarried.' But I said, 'Awesome!'" She laughs. "'You found the problem and now we can fix it!'"

Lindsay was excited, but Jordan took the news hard.

"I felt terrible," he says. "She survived. She did everything she could to preserve her fertility so she was one hundred percent able to have children, and then I come along, we're in love with each other, and then I'm the cause for her to go through another challenge to accomplish her dream."

Both were astounded by the odds of two people meeting and getting married who had such unique fertility challenges. They were also immensely grateful there was a potential solution, one that had just launched in the medical market. Science now allowed for the ability to create embryos, suck one cell out of each, and check them under a microscope to determine which embryos were genetically normal. So that's what the pair did. In June 2005, they began IVF utilizing pre-implantation genetic diagnosis, or PGD. Alas, no good embryos. But in September, three healthy embryos were identified and two were implanted in Lindsay. The doctor told them that if this didn't work, the next step could be a sperm donor. Lindsay's frozen eggs were available, but success was unlikely in the reproductive process due to Jordan's chromosomal abnormality. Miraculously, this time, Lindsay got pregnant. With cautious optimism, they counted the days, praying she wouldn't miscarry. At five weeks, Dr. Rosenwaks told them they could come in to see the fetal heartbeat.

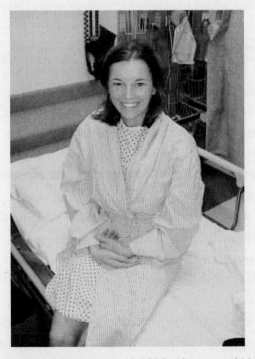

Lindsay, undergoing IVF treatment in 2005. (Courtesy of Lindsay Beck)

"So we're there, and Dr. Rosenwaks cautioned us, 'If there's no heartbeat, it's still early, don't panic.' He was trying to manage our expectations," she says. "And there is a little jelly bean with a heartbeat. The moment was surreal, and I remember saying, 'This is why I wanted to survive.' I can still picture it: I'm in the stirrups, Jordan is by my head, Dr. Rosenwaks is literally between my legs, and we're all looking at this little TV screen, and despite that completely exposed moment, it was so calm and peaceful and happy. And I was thinking, *This is what I want for all the people I'm trying to help*. It was really, really powerful."

The pregnancy went smoothly, although Lindsay was nervous about the health of the baby. Her ob-gyn calmed her nerves by categorizing Lindsay as a perfectly healthy mom-to-be.

"And I laughed, 'What? Have you seen my chart?' And she said, 'I know it's been a long haul to get here, but from a pregnancy standpoint, you're a normal, healthy patient.' I would still be nervous for all the tests and ultrasounds, and I remember she said, 'Welcome to motherhood. It's a lifetime of worry.' It made me feel like I was acting normal, and this is how you're supposed to feel."

Their healthy daughter Paisley was born on June 1, 2006. Lindsay and Jordan were delighted to keep the gender of their new baby a surprise.

She says, smiling, "We joked that it was the one thing we could do the old-fashioned way."

Their joy was paired with a sense of wonder. Both had beaten the odds to have a biological child.

"For both of us, it was magical."

When Paisley was just hours old, Dr. Rosenwaks came for a visit at the hospital.

"And I asked him, 'How long after you stop nursing do you have to wait before doing IVF again?' He said, 'Okay, that's a record. No one has ever asked me minutes after delivery when they can have another.' But I couldn't help but think, *I want to do this again and again and again.*"

Lindsay shared the news with Nancy, who made it clear she did not want to be called Grandma.

"I told Nancy and her partner Dr. Hartman," she says, "'Not only did you save my life, you enabled this. My legacy. This baby was born because of you.'"

Busy new mom Lindsay continued her work with Fertile Hope. She coauthored a guideline issued by the American Society of Clinical Oncology. Published in the *Journal of Clinical Oncology,* the ASCO guideline reads in part: "As part of education and informed consent prior to cancer therapy, oncologists should address the possibility of infertility with patients treated during their reproductive years and be prepared to discuss possible fertility preservation options or refer appropriate and interested patients to reproductive specialists."

This was a huge step forward in Lindsay's mission to ensure that cancer patients were made aware that their fertility was potentially at risk and that options were available to preserve it. Now, instead of Fertile Hope making calls, the foundation's phones were ringing nonstop. Doctors and cancer centers around the country began inviting Fertile Hope representatives to grand rounds; patients now had to be informed, so physicians were reaching out for information and guidance.

Lindsay also coauthored a book called *100 Questions & Answers About Cancer and Fertility.* It featured practical and credible answers to the most common questions asked by cancer patients and survivors about fertility.

"I cowrote it with a physician because I felt like I needed the MD expertise and endorsement," she says.

The first person Lindsay hired at Fertile Hope, a fellow cancer survivor and passionate advocate, also worked as a coauthor of the book.

Work and family were keeping Lindsay busy as she and Jordan cared for seven-month-old Paisley. And it was about to get busier; ideally, they wanted their family to grow by one. Lindsay stopped breastfeeding in December and began IVF treatments in February 2007. The results were discouraging times two. The first cycle didn't work and the second resulted in an early miscarriage. Dr. Rosenwaks told her to take the summer off from IVF treatments. Lindsay grudgingly agreed but made sure to chart her ovulation schedule and not miss an opportunity.

"It was my only coping mechanism," she says. "*We'll take the summer off from IVF, but I'll secretly have us try on our own.*"

She tried and succeeded. Lindsay got pregnant and gave birth to a healthy son, Walker, on March 20, 2008. She took a three-month maternity leave from Fertile Hope and returned to work in July. The foundation was gearing up for a productive fall fund-raising season. But as it approached, the very month that would typically generate big dollars instead revealed big trouble. On September 15, 2008, Lehman Brothers filed for Chapter 11 bankruptcy protection. The collapse was very bad news for the global financial markets and for Fertile Hope. The people who supported the foundation were greatly impacted by the financial-market meltdown. Although Jordan had left his job at Lehman a year earlier for another job on Wall Street, many of his friends still worked at the now-bankrupt financial-services firm.

"New York City supported Fertile Hope," she says. "All of Jordan's friends and clients were the ones who came and bid on everything at the auctions. Wall Street supported Fertile Hope big-time, and so that was devastating. I thought, *What do we do?*"

TEN YEARS LATER

In early 2009, Lindsay began to reflect on the quality of her life, something she'd so passionately fought for back in 1999. She was still alive ten years after her first cancer diagnosis, she'd formed a meaningful and important foundation, she'd met the man of her dreams, and she had given birth to two children. Now she was working four ten-hour days just so she could be a full-time mom on Fridays. Even with a full-time nanny, she was feeling out of sorts and out of touch with the core business she had birthed.

"I had two kids in New York City, the fund-raising market was dreadful, and I was really tired of running a small business," she says. "I want to help patients, but at this point I felt like a glorified administrator. I was doing HR, and accounting, and managing my employees, and I hated it. And I'm leaving my kids and not loving the job. I knew I had to fix it."

Lindsay began also to notice other groups popping up that addressed fertility protection for cancer patients. Packets and information kits were being given to doctors and patients.

"At first I was feeling a loss of control, and *What is going on? How are we losing market share?*" she says. "And then I had this lightbulb moment. *We've done it! We've succeeded! All along, all I've wanted is for everyone to talk about fertility. I wanted it to become standard practice. I wanted it embedded in everything that people normally do. And now it is.*"

That's when the last line of her original business plan came to the front of her mind. Back in 2001, when she launched Fertile Hope, Lindsay knew someday the foundation would be run by someone else. Her plan ends with the following words: "Ultimately, it will not make sense for this to be a stand-alone organization. It should be part of a larger cancer experience. Once the problem is solved, we should be acquired."

In March 2009, Lindsay flew to Austin, Texas, on Walker's first birthday and presented the idea of a Fertile Hope acquisition to the Lance Armstrong Foundation.

"They said yes," she says with a smile.

Lindsay set about the exciting process of the merger and acquisition, which was finalized in July. She joined the Lance Armstrong Foundation, serving as an adviser and consultant. Her role was to work with major health insurance companies as well as self-insured corporations. Lindsay would meet with chief medical officers or heads of human resources and make her pitch.

"I say, 'Here's a business case for the benefit. I think you should cover fertility preservation for cancer patients, and here's why it makes sense for both patients and payers.'"

Working and raising two active kids in a small New York City apartment began to wear on Lindsay. There was also the emotional toll from another round of IVF treatments; the action plan was in motion for a third child. She told Jordan it was time to move to San Francisco and find a house with a yard. In September, Jordan's boss told him of a job opportunity in the Bay Area and he jumped at it. The Becks were in their California home by Christmas.

Following two IVF cycles with Dr. Alan Copperman, a fertility specialist at Mount Sinai Medical Center, Lindsay gave birth to baby Scarlett on April 6, 2011. She and Dr. Copperman had worked together for years through Fertile Hope. When the doctor called Lindsay with word that she was pregnant, the moment was powerful. After Nancy heard the news, she sent Lindsay a charm.

"I said, 'Lindsay, this has nothing to do with the kids. This is all about you. This present's for you.' While I do celebrate her children, that was *her* dream. My dream as her physician is to celebrate her."

Jordan, one-week-old Scarlett, Paisley, Lindsay, Walker.
Mill Valley, California, 2011. (Credit: Michelle Walker Photography)

Now nearly thirty-five years old, Lindsay began to wonder what was next for her professionally.

"Once you've had a career driven by passion," she says, "what do you do next? How do you repeat that? Some people never have that, and I had it at twenty-four. How do you do it again? What does that look like?"

When Scarlett was six weeks old, Lindsay took a step toward laying the foundation for her future. She entered Wharton's San Francisco Executive MBA program. Classes are held every other Friday and Saturday for two years straight. She continues to work from home for the Lance Armstrong Foundation.

"It's almost the perfect school for working moms. The kids barely know I'm gone. Two Saturdays a month they have Daddy Day, but I feel like that's a dad's job regardless." She laughs. "Even if I wasn't in school that might be happening."

Lindsay will graduate in May 2013 with a full MBA. She loves the opportunity the program offers for global study.

"Over Christmas break I went to Africa for a week and took a leadership class in Rwanda to learn about how Rwanda's leader achieved such remarkable change, from genocide to prosperity," she explains. "We met with leaders and asked, 'How do you do this?' We then brought that information back home and asked, 'Anyone can be a leader when things are good, but when things are bad, what do you do and how do you do it? What could be worse than genocide?' Any corporation I'm going to run will never have that baggage."

Lindsay's contract with the Lance Armstrong Foundation is from year to year, which allows her the potential for change.

"I'll always be involved. I'll always be on the advisory board and advise them on fertility-related issues, but they're so nice and so flexible on if and how we work together over time," she says. "It's a really rare, rare opportunity. I feel very fortunate."

Good fortune has been part of Lindsay's life story. Nancy credits her with tremendous drive and courage, but Lindsay knew of four other young tongue cancer patients receiving radiation treatments at the same time she did at the University of California in San Francisco. Only Lindsay survived.

"Lindsay's the lucky one," says Nancy. "I don't know if she'll ever know how lucky she was. Even if you have the best surgeon in the world, there's nothing like a little luck with it."

I ask Nancy, now that thirteen years have passed since Lindsay's first cancer diagnosis, what Lindsay's medical future holds.

"I think she can look forward to what kind of grandmother she wants to be," Nancy says.

For the first time in eight years, Lindsay is not taking fertility drugs, nursing, or pregnant. She's leaving the plan this time to chance.

"I've done ten IVF cycles. I don't want to pay for any more, I don't want to endure any more, but it's hard to say, 'My goal was four or five.'" She laughs. "Not to achieve a goal just does not go over very well for me. But, I think we've agreed, no more IVF, but we're still on the fence about if we would be open to another miracle."

When I ask her how she manages to find balance in her very busy life (which requires spreadsheets for weekly menu planning and activities), she pops me another Nancy-ism.

"Nancy always says, 'You'll never find balance. If that's the goal you'll always fail.' She says you can still have it all, just not all at the same time," Lindsay explains. "She says, 'You have crystal balls and rubber balls, and you're always juggling everything, and you have to identify in the moment which is a rubber ball and which is a crystal ball. Juggle them all, but don't drop the crystal balls.' I find myself living by those imperatives—*Okay, what are the crystal balls today, or this week, or this month?*, and for me those things are vacation, or family time, or my special dates with the kids, and I'm not willing to compromise them. You have to make sure, too, when you're in a crystal ball moment, that you're present, not half in. I don't want to be at the park with my kids on my cell phone trying to work."

Those busy mental wheels, always spinning inside Lindsay's head. Her constant forward movement fueled by action plans has left her with a full life and, ironically, some apprehension about reaching the finish line too soon.

"When Nancy diagnosed me, when she sent me home with the pen and paper, I made a Bucket List. *What do I want to do if I'm going to die?* Ten years later, everything on that list is done except for one thing," she laughs. "And I'm afraid to do the last thing because that means I can die."

Lindsay makes me ask what the last thing is, as if sharing it out loud means she's one step closer to accomplishing it.

"A safari in Africa. Jordan says, 'Let's go!' But I say, 'No, no, no.' It's like looking over the edge at the great big black hole."

Lindsay may never go on safari, but there's a good chance her daughter Paisley will. One of Lindsay's dreams for her kids is that they see the world. Before she went to Rwanda for the MBA program, Lindsay showed her kids where Africa is on a globe. Now their little mental wheels are spinning.

"Right now, in my house, our living room is set up like an airplane. All the dining room chairs are lined up in a row and there's a food cart in the back and they bring the food out to each other," she describes. "They have a steering wheel in the front, and every day they pick out a place on the globe where they're going. Paisley asks me, 'When I'm ten can I go to Australia?'" And she says, 'When I go on my honey trip'—that's what she calls a honeymoon—'I want to go to Africa.' And I feel like, that's what I want for them: a happy life of adventure and experience. You can come home to a comfortable place that you've earned and worked hard for, but you should know that the whole world isn't that way."

Clearly, the world of medicine isn't the same since Lindsay set out on her unplanned expedition. At just thirty-five years old, she is a pioneer.

"Lindsay changed modern medicine," says Nancy. "I think she will go down as one of the most heroic game changers in cancer treatment bar none. She's right up there, to me, with some of the big doctors who have done some of the most innovative science."

You can't help but wonder, *What will this amazing girl do next?* I ask her what message she thinks she's left behind so far in her journey.

"My message is, if something is important to you, fight for it. Don't just accept the this-is-how-we-do-it approach," she says. "Every time you hit a roadblock or are unhappy or you get a no, there's usually a way around, or over, or under, or whatever. If it's important to you, fight for it. I feel like my role now is to be an agent of change in the world."

How fascinating it will be to see what Lindsay's fighting to change ten years from now.

PATRICK WEILAND

When I was hired in 1998 as a correspondent for *Dateline NBC*, Patrick Weiland was a three-year veteran producer. A superstar. His skills were unmatched. You had to stand in line to have Patrick assigned as a producer to your story. He could land, like few others, the elusive who, what, and where that a piece demanded. I was based in New York and he in Los Angeles, so we never had the chance to work together. I did cross paths with him a lot at 30 Rock when he was working in the city. Then, over the years, I would describe Patrick's departure from the network as a slow fade. He didn't just leave abruptly one day; he came and went, managing what most of us thought were garden-variety demons. We saw plenty of that at work and in our own private lives. Only when I sat down to hear Patrick's complete journey did I realize how far he actually fell, and what a superstar he truly is.

❖

Patrick Weiland was born in May 1963 in Minneapolis, Minnesota. His family moved to nearby Bloomington when he was four, contributing to a population boom sparked by a business boom under way in the city. Two major interstates were complete and every major sports

team in Minnesota played within the city limits. Bloomington offered the Weilands a suburban lifestyle along with a lush playground
dotted with parks, rivers, and lakes. Patrick grew up like many of us,
lucky enough to think back on barefoot summers, unlocked front
doors, and good, clean, dirty fun.

"I had a dirt bike before I had a bicycle," he says with a grin.

Patrick and his three sisters grew up riding farm tractors, dipping
toes in the chilly waters of Lake Superior, and packing up the family
van for annual camping trips to Gooseberry Falls State Park in Minnesota and Glacier National Park in Montana. The Weiland family
photo book is filled with Kodak moments that capture a wonderfully
typical childhood. Snap! Four barefoot kids, sitting atop a wooden
sign that reads LEAVING BLACKFEET INDIAN RESERVATION, with a back-
drop of snowcapped mountains. Ron Weiland worked as the head
of technology for Minnesota's newspaper the *Star Tribune*. His wife,
Mary, was a radiation therapist. Together they provided a fun and loving home for their four children, Maggie, Anamaria, Patrick, and Sue.

"My parents didn't have a lot of money," he says, "but we never
felt that."

Patrick was closest to his youngest sister, Sue, who was just three
and a half years younger than him. She loved the outdoors and from
an early age felt a kinship with animals. She always had a shoebox
full of rescued baby squirrels or raccoons that she was bottle-feeding.
Her love of nature was matched by her love for adventure. Patrick
writes about Sue in the family photo book:

> *When her seven-year-old brother suggested she might just be the*
> *right size to jump off the garage roof with an umbrella and float to*
> *the ground like Mary Poppins, at four years old, Sue was game. She'd*
> *already mastered scrambling onto the roof without any help from*
> *me. The only casualty of our stunt was Mom's nerves; she never got*

over the sight of her toddler—umbrella in hand—poised at the peak
of the roof.

After high school, Patrick enrolled at the University of Minnesota. Sue's sense of adventure was equaled by Patrick's sense of curiosity. He was drawn to science courses and planned to go on to medical school. He began working at the University of Minnesota Medical School to help pay for college. His dad was ecstatic at the idea of a future doctor in the family. Patrick completed the coursework for premed, but in his final year at U of M, he needed to balance out his science-heavy course load. Four classes would do the trick; he could graduate with a journalism degree. The curriculum required Patrick to intern at a local television station, so he chose the CBS affiliate in Minneapolis, WCCO-TV.

"They were doing an undercover report on home health care," Patrick explains, "and I knew medical records inside and out. So I did all the research and I was the undercover person who went in and did all the undercover footage."

When the segment aired, WCCO gave Patrick credit as a researcher in the report.

"They called me, like about six months later, and said, 'You won a Peabody Award,'" Patrick says, shaking his head. "And I was like, 'What is that? Is that like a Professor Peabody Award?' I didn't know what a Peabody was!"

Imagine one of the highest awards in your business. That's a Peabody for electronic media. The only honor more prestigious than a George Foster Peabody Award is an Alfred I. duPont–Columbia University Award. A twenty-two-year-old winning a Peabody was unprecedented. In 1986, Patrick graduated from college, and WCCO hired him full-time as a producer in their investigative unit. He decided to delay medical school for a year.

"And so I just fell in love with it," he says. Patrick was 100 percent in.

Dad was not. While supportive, he was concerned about Patrick's future.

"He said to me, 'You'll never make more than twelve thousand dollars a year!'" Patrick grins, thinking back. "And so when I went to the network and was making about ninety-five thousand dollars, or something like that, my parents were both like . . ." His eyes pop, mimicking their reaction.

His sister Sue's life was not unfolding with similar promise. After high school, she attended a community college for about a year but dropped out when she began dating a Minnesota outdoorsman ten years her senior. Those decisions, over time, would prove to affect Sue's relationship with her brother and her entire family.

In early 1993, after years of working at WCCO, Patrick received a call from the network. CBS in New York was launching a prime time newsmagazine in the spring called *Eye to Eye with Connie Chung*. They flew in Patrick to interview for the job of producer. He would be at least ten years younger than the other producers on staff. The kid from Bloomington was headed for the Big Apple. The idea of a fresh and exciting start in a big city prompted Patrick, now twenty-nine, to consider "coming out" professionally about his sexuality. He'd told his family in his early twenties that he was gay and had received their full support, but he'd not let anyone in his work life know about his partner of more than a decade.

"When I was moving to New York, I thought, *Well, I'm gonna come out in my final meeting before they offer me the job.*"

Looking back, Patrick marvels at the way ignorance and fearlessness often cohabitate in the brain. Sitting with Connie Chung and two other power players on staff, Patrick made the decision.

"So, they said, 'Is there anything else you need to say?' And I

looked at Connie and I said, 'Well, yes, there actually is,'" Patrick
continues. "'I'm gonna bring my partner with me from Minneapolis.'"

Crickets? Awkward silence?

Hardly.

"Connie Chung put her hand firmly on the middle of my thigh,
looked directly at me, and said, 'That's just faaaaaaantastic,'" Patrick
says with a huge smile. "It was the first time I had come out and I was
so nervous, so it was just great."

Patrick was a producer for *Eye to Eye* from 1993 until the program ended in 1995. He was immediately recruited by executives
from *Dateline NBC,* who were rebuilding the investigative unit and
knew Patrick was a thirty-two-year-old phenom. He did not disap-
point. Consistently exceptional work for years made Patrick a valued
and respected part of the *Dateline* team.

Patrick, Peggy Holter, Keith Morrison, Polly Powell, John Reiss.
1998 Emmy Awards, New York City. (Courtesy of Malachy Wienges)

In the fall of 1998, Patrick once again landed the hardware to back up his stellar reputation. He'd already been awarded a Peabody, several Edward R. Murrow Awards, and a highly coveted Livingston Award, given to an exceptional journalist younger than thirty-five. He would now add two national Emmy Awards for *Dateline* pieces he'd produced, to be presented at a ceremony in New York City. Patrick and his partner made the flight from Los Angeles to New York for the exciting event. But, also on board, like an invisible oxygen mask dangling in front of them, was a loose end.

"I had to go get a test," says Patrick.

Before leaving for New York, Patrick took an HIV test, but the results would not be available until he returned home. Committed partners of sixteen years, the two were devastated by the possibility of an HIV diagnosis. On the evening of the awards, Patrick won two Emmys for *Dateline* and celebrated with his coworkers and colleagues. The next day, the partners flew back to L.A. where the test results awaited.

"I was in shock," he says softly.

The doctor told Patrick that his white blood cell count was manageable, but the amount of human immunodeficiency virus active in his bloodstream was off the charts. He was a very sick thirty-five-year-old man.

"I didn't talk to anyone about it, which was a huge mistake." He shakes his head. "I was ashamed. There's still an enormous social stigma that's attached to HIV, even within the gay community. It's something you have to live with the rest of your life. Growing up when I did, you had a sense of shame about your sexuality. It took me so long to gain the comfort of being openly gay and being accepted for who I am. It was a struggle, ever since I was a teen, and then to contract HIV on top of it—it was devastatingly difficult."

Patrick's doctor immediately prescribed a drug cocktail so the virus would be held at bay. What was not minimized was Patrick's overwhelming sense of embarrassment, fear, and hopelessness. Those emotions were full-blown; they dominated his mental being. He was struggling with the idea that his body was being invaded by a preventable illness, and that the consequence could be deadly. When an acquaintance suggested Patrick try methamphetamine to control his anxiety, the guy who never did drugs, who'd tried marijuana in college but didn't like it, smoked his first glass pipe full of crystal meth.

"Within a week, I had the HIV diagnosis, I had won two Emmys, and I had tried crystal meth." He pauses. "The highest high, the lowest low."

Patrick says he was addicted from the first hit. His searing humiliation was replaced with euphoria.

"I forgot every care I had in the world. Loved it," he says. "I thought, *I'm dying now anyway, who cares?*"

The producer extraordinaire was now an illegal-drug user. Patrick says the term "binge user" would describe his pattern. He'd get high on Friday after work and use throughout the weekend.

"I was very disciplined. I was a high-functioning user. I would never take it while I was working," Patrick explains. "I needed something. I was living in such pain, and that was the drug I chose. And I was hooked from the first minute because it worked."

His close friend Margaret Bailey, a fellow producer for *Eye to Eye*, was living in New York City when Patrick learned of his HIV and when he began taking drugs. On the opposite coast in L.A., Patrick could hide the dark side of his life from Margaret and talk to her as if everything was okay.

"We had other friends who were concerned, but it was very hard to get a handle on it," says Margaret. "Friends had noticed Patrick had lost weight and that he did not stay in touch regularly. I had little bitty kids, I had a life full of distraction, and I was worried and far away, and I felt very powerless."

Despite doctors telling Patrick they were managing the virus, he was convinced he was dying and that he was damaged goods. After he and his partner broke up in 2000, Patrick began to see less of his friends and use more of the meth. He eventually had to share with his bosses at *Dateline* that he'd tested positive for HIV.

"I was missing work a lot. I said I wasn't feeling well. Blamed it on my HIV. I used that as an excuse," he admits, "and when you have that, y'know, no one's gonna challenge you."

In 2003, Patrick's superiors at NBC were concerned enough about his performance that they coordinated an intervention. His mom and a family friend were flown to L.A., and in the home of dear friends, they confronted Patrick about his drug use. The plan worked; he agreed to get treatment. Patrick says NBC could not have been more caring and accommodating. His family was just as supportive. Everyone was willing to pave the way for Patrick's road to recovery.

Nearly two thousand miles away, in northwest Wisconsin, Patrick's sister Sue was battling her own demons: alcohol and a physically abusive relationship with her longtime boyfriend, Peter Whyte. Patrick's parents, who had divorced when he was in college but were still close friends, had tried for years to convince Sue to leave Peter. So had Patrick and his sisters. Still, she remained with him, her first and only boyfriend. They lived together in a cabin at the hook of the Apple River, about twelve miles from her mother's cabin on Paulson Lake.

"I thought he was a jerk. I knew right away," says Patrick with disdain. "How he spoke to her, how he treated her. Big, lumbering, muscular guy."

Sue very rarely reported to authorities the injuries she sustained over the years at the hands of Peter. When she sought treatment for her broken ribs, and other injuries too horrific to share here, Sue hopscotched to various area hospitals to avoid developing a consistent charting of abuse. The family was aware of Sue's bruises and black eyes, and continually begged her to leave Peter. The abuse would abate for several years and then, literally, kick back in.

Peter's presence strained Sue's relationship with Patrick and the rest of the family. In the years before and during Patrick's addiction, he'd argue with Sue about the family's precious time spent together.

"There would be fights about the fact that I didn't want Peter at Thanksgiving or Christmas. I told him, 'I don't want you around. We love our sister and we just can't have you around,'" he remembers. "Then she would say, 'No, no, please. I just want everybody to get along.' Y'know, I'd come home for four days and I was like, 'Okay.'"

Patrick's personal life was just as erratic. His work-sanctioned stints in rehab became a roller coaster of success and failure. He'd spend weeks in an isolated rehab environment, then opt instead for an outpatient program. He was in and out of twelve-step programs. For six months he'd beat the meth, but then succumb again to its numbing allure.

"There is something to be said for the theory that you can't force someone to get clean until they're ready," he explains.

In early 2005, Patrick was "clean" and back at *Dateline* to produce stories surrounding the trial of pop superstar Michael Jackson, who had been accused of child molestation. Patrick was convinced he could do the work. But, again, he had misjudged the power of the drug. Patrick says his "sick brain" convinced him that NBC and his friends were "better off without this piece of shit." He couldn't imagine why they would be angry if he didn't stay at work or keep in touch. Patrick further withdrew from his life.

Margaret and other close friends had no idea Patrick was living with such a heavy burden. He had disconnected from the very people who would have reached out to help. But the addicted Patrick could not believe that. Why would people want him in their life now? He felt the only thing acting in his best interest was meth. He didn't need anyone else.

"I used to always come back to this metaphor in my head, that I was a balloon on a tether," he says as his fingers strum the air, "and I was plucking off the ropes, one by one, and then I would just float away."

And float he did. Patrick took yet another extended leave of absence from *Dateline*. In December 2005, the company offered a buyout to various employees, and Patrick took it. His leave had now become permanent. The wily addiction pounced. Patrick stopped smoking meth and began to inject it.

"I learned it in rehab; go figure. I didn't know you could do that! Fantastic!" he says sarcastically. "I can get really high now!"

The high is faster, and eventually, deadlier.

"It'll kill you," Patrick confirms. "It's one hundred percent terminal."

Hopeless and blinded by his addiction, Patrick was acutely aware of the bizarre path his life had taken.

"I kept a clean house, I still had my nice car, but I was a wreck. I was connecting with drug dealers in locations that would be drug dens that you think of in a movie. I had covered these stories. I knew what I was doing. I acted like a producer," he says, throwing his hands up in amazement, "and I knew I was killing myself."

Patrick says at the time, he was actually okay with the reality of certain death. He had tried everything to get clean. Trying to have hope seemed hopeless.

"I could not imagine that my life could ever get back to the highs of where it was. I had blown it." He says the dialogue in his head was, *What does it matter anymore? This is the only relief I can find.*

Patrick's addiction was draining, spiritually and financially. He was spending substantial amounts of money on drugs and material things. Looking back, he says the splurging was perhaps an attempt to reassure everyone that he was doing well.

In May 2006, Patrick decided to spend $25,000 renovating the kitchen in his mother's house on Paulson Lake in northwest Wisconsin, just a dozen miles from the cabin where Sue lived with Peter. Patrick thoroughly enjoyed spending time with his mother and Sue, and he valued the chance to stay busy with a creative project. Summer days at the lake were productive and meaningful, but when Patrick traveled back to L.A. every few weeks, he continued to get high. Despondent, he also stopped taking his HIV medications.

"I just didn't even care," Patrick says. "That was the saddest part."

One month later, in June, some positive news came. Sue had finally found the courage to leave Peter. They'd been together for nearly two troubled, alcohol-fueled, abusive decades.

"She had just finished a nursing program and was working at a nursing home," Patrick explains. "She had started to develop enough outside relationships where she felt secure enough. And he seemed okay with it."

Sue moved in with their mom, and for the first time since they were kids, Patrick and his sister spent quality time under the same roof. They negotiated who got what room and shared a closet. Renovations on the house, and ideally Sue's life, were in full swing.

"In August, I was home for the last sort of wrap-up stuff on the kitchen, and I couldn't believe how civil everyone was," Patrick recalls.

Sue and Peter were in the final stages of separating their finances and belongings. The pair talked frequently but agreed he should not see her. Things seemed so good that threats of filing a restraining order against Peter were dropped. Patrick reached out to him.

"I left a message for him saying, 'Thank you. I'm impressed with the way you've handled things, and I'm glad to hear you're at peace with it.'"

In mid-August, Sue agreed to go on a group camping trip with Peter and friends. The pair had a peaceful, platonic trip.

A few mornings later, on the front porch of the lake house, Patrick, Sue, and their mom were enjoying coffee. Patrick decided to pull out an article he'd brought, never thinking they'd have time to discuss it. He'd had it for months and popped it in his briefcase before leaving L.A. The story was titled "Life Is Empty and Meaningless." He thought the deeper meaning of the story—that you *make* life full and meaningful—would encourage Sue to continue her healthy direction. The topic sparked a uniquely open conversation; the three told each other what mattered to them and how much they valued one another.

"We got to say, 'I love you, your life is meaningful, I'm so happy,'" Patrick says.

That Thursday, August 18, Patrick returned to L.A. Sue called him the next day, ending the phone call with, "I love you, Pat." He now considers the chance to say, "I love you, too, Sue," a gift. He would never talk to his sister again.

Sue, sitting on the dock at her house along the Apple River. Somerset, Wisconsin, 2006. (Courtesy of Patrick Weiland)

On Saturday, August 20, Sue went back to the river cabin to pick up a few of her remaining belongings. Friends were boating on a dammed section of the river, enjoying the afternoon; she joined in. So did Peter. The relaxing gathering turned into a day of drinking. That evening, Sue and Peter ended up in their cabin. A neighbor heard them arguing in the early-morning hours.

"At two o'clock in the morning, they got into an argument," Patrick says with disdain, "and he slit her throat. He stabbed her nineteen times, one time for every year of their relationship."

The horrific scene inside the trashed cabin indicated a long and violent struggle. Sue, nine inches shorter than Peter and half his weight, had fought back. While the autopsy indicated Sue had a black eye, broken nose, and eight fatal stab wounds, Peter told the 911 operator that Sue had attacked him. He was sitting in a chair when authorities arrived at 7:20 Sunday morning, claiming injuries to his wrist and abdomen proved he'd acted in self-defense.

That Sunday morning, Patrick's unknowing mother was enjoying the lake view from her porch with friends.

Patrick recalls, "The sheriff's deputies were walking up the driveway and she knew." He snaps his fingers. "She picked up the phone and called me and said, 'Sue's been murdered.'"

Patrick spent the next twelve hours calling his sisters, father, friends, and relatives. He immediately enlisted journalist friends in the Minneapolis market to cover the story of his sister's murder.

"Because I knew—rural homicide, domestic," he explains from the perspective of a veteran news producer. "If it doesn't get coverage, the police don't thoroughly investigate."

Patrick then called the county sheriff to give him the family's permission to talk to the local news media. His goal was to enlist the help of the state crime lab instead of the local coroner, who often has limited resources to process lab work. As the family would learn over the months, the Wisconsin State Crime Laboratory was also understaffed, causing a four-month delay in the trial, and horrifically, a thirteen-month stay in the county morgue for Sue's body. The Weilands wanted desperately to bury Sue but also wanted her body to be available if additional evidence needed to be collected.

"My parents couldn't bury their daughter. It was like watching them get beaten with baseball bats," Patrick says. "It was torture. Absolute torture."

Patrick's mom, Mary, expressed her anguish to the Minneapolis newspaper where Patrick's father had worked, the *Star Tribune*. An excerpt from the article reads, "'I'm falling apart about this,' said Weiland's mother, Mary. 'But we don't want to do anything to jeopardize the prosecution.'"

The scheduled May trial was delayed until September. Patrick continued to travel back and forth between L.A. and Wisconsin. He says he never used drugs during his stays in Wisconsin; his focus was to exhaust every opportunity to advocate for his sister.

"That's the one thing I felt I could do. That was my purpose," he says. "I think that's what kept me alive during that time."

But Patrick was closer to death than ever, by his own hand. He was not taking his HIV drugs and during trips back to L.A. was often bingeing on meth, the drug that so expertly soothed his pain.

"I was in a free fall. I would have periods of clarity and periods where I was very on, but then I would binge and disappear from everyone for six weeks in L.A.," he says. "I'd go to AA meetings, I'd stay clean for a week or three weeks, and then I'd get home and I'd lock myself up in the house and use. I don't know how I survived it. It was bad."

Finally, in September 2007, thirteen months after Sue's death, the trial of Peter G. Whyte began. Each morning, the Weiland sisters put one sunflower, Sue's favorite, in a vase outside the courthouse. After two weeks of proceedings, the jury made its decision.

"I've never been so tense in my life," Patrick says, shaking his head with raised eyebrows. "It was hell."

The jury did not believe Whyte had acted in self-defense and convicted him of second-degree intentional homicide. A first step toward justice for Sue.

The family's next pressure cooker was the sentencing. A month later, KARE-TV, the NBC affiliate in the Twin Cities, covered the sentencing hearing. Videotape shows Sue's sisters and one of her nieces describing their loss to the presiding judge. Middle sister Anamaria simply says, "We remain devastated."

The judge imposed a sentence that ensured that fifty-four-year-old Whyte would most likely be incarcerated until he died: forty years in a maximum-security prison in Wisconsin.

"After the conviction, I went into a one-month . . ." Patrick's palm glides downward. "I don't even know what happened. I remember vividly after a binge, with bloody arms, and being sick, I remember lying there thinking, *Okay, when I close my eyes the next time I'm not going to wake up. I think I'm gonna go. This is the knife's edge.*"

Patrick says it was on that proverbial edge that, oddly, his mind became sharp for an instant. Sue entered his thoughts—his beautiful sister, whose death was preventable. In the days ahead, he would realize that he and Sue had been living a similar story.

"She could not escape for whatever reason, and I couldn't escape. I was just like a battered woman with the drug," he says. "I was in the same helpless, hopeless, powerless situation, but my attacker was the drug I was doing."

Patrick said that for the first time, his thinking changed. He realized he could not put his family through another catastrophic loss.

"It saved my life, in the end. In the end, on that knife's edge, I knew that watching my parents and the people who love my parents suffer from Sue's death," says Patrick, "I knew that I could not die."

In January 2008, Patrick set about the business of living, with no savings remaining and no medical insurance to buy HIV medication. He was in very rough shape: weak, extremely thin, no appetite.

"I moved home to my family and lay in my mother's house for months," Patrick says. "I had no strength to summon all of the wreckage I had caused in my life, and the tremendous loss of Sue. But I was never going to use again. I was determined."

After four months, Patrick sought medical help from a community center in Minneapolis. Staff there made it possible for him to see a doctor who prescribed a series of HIV drugs. He told Patrick his chances for survival.

"He said, 'You have a fifty-fifty six-month mortality. That means fifty percent of the people who are in the condition you are in will not be alive in six months.' And that took my breath away," Patrick recalls, "because I was clean at that point for five months."

There was no plan. Patrick simply spent time with close friends in Minneapolis and healed his body. He opted out of meds that were suggested for depression.

"I was gonna be miserable. And depressed," he says logically. "I needed to be depressed. I *was* depressed. There was a reason I was depressed. And I needed to make the changes in my life and reengineer my life."

To say a switch flipped in Patrick's brain discredits the amount of mental muscle he already applied to his recovery; he'd made many attempts to recover over the years. But, he does say, the pairing of devastating loss with genuine gratitude acted as kindling and a match; they ignited his changed thinking. He now saw himself as worthy of repair.

"I do believe in the power of the mind. It is a powerful, powerful tool. All you have to do is change your frame of reference and the way you're thinking, but it's a long and slow process," he says. "Do I feel like damaged goods? I don't. And that is a miracle."

TEN YEARS LATER

In the fall of 2008, ten years after Patrick's HIV diagnosis and crystal meth addiction, he received a call from a former colleague who runs a production company in Minnesota. She'd developed a successful show for the Travel Channel and needed a freelance field producer. With no idea that Patrick had struggled with addiction, she offered him the job. Coincidentally, the host of *Bizarre Foods with Andrew Zimmern* is himself a recovering drug addict of twenty years.

Bizarre Foods features the kind of far-out fare that makes people both squirm and tune in by the millions in seventy-two countries around the world. As field producer and director for the program, Patrick always has a bag packed. It's routine for him to travel to Amsterdam, Tokyo, Bangkok, Rio de Janeiro, and Montreal within three months. The show has also bellied up to the bizarre in Namibia, Hong Kong, Finland, Argentina, Nicaragua, Germany, Greece, Italy, and the jungles of Southeast Asia.

"I had a bucket with two hundred fifty tarantulas in the back of my car, and I'm not a spider person," Patrick says, recalling a trip to Cambodia. The crew tagged along on a tarantula-trapping trip. The hairy spiders are defanged, deep-fried, and sold as snacks at roadside stands.

Patrick, field producing on the set of *Bizarre Foods with Andrew Zimmern*. Austin, Texas, 2011. (Courtesy of Alex Needles)

"I couldn't eat the tarantulas," he says, defeated, "even though they were fresh."

At forty-nine, Patrick says he's excited about his professional future, and is personally joyful and physically strong. He embraces not only who he is now, but who he has been—all of it.

I then ask the question you have to ask recovering addicts. After all, I know he's asked himself. It's been four years.

"Do you worry about a relapse?"

Patrick answers that he does not, saying, "You always have to remember your lowest point, and mine is so tangible and so present in my sister's murder that I can instantly access that pain and use that."

Cold, hard facts are effective, too.

"I know with absolute certainty," he says, "if I use, I die. Addiction specialists say relapsing addicts pick right back up where they left their habit, no matter how long they managed to stay clean. In my case, the amounts would be deadly. So, for me getting clean and staying clean meant I had to change. I had to choose to want to live. Even on my worst days—and they happen—I am so grateful to be alive and present."

Would he change the murderous events of August 20, 2006? Of course, but, clearly, the hole in his heart from losing Sue is shaped like a halo.

"If my sister hadn't died, I would have died. I have no doubt about that." Patrick begins to cry. "She struggled with her alcoholism, and she struggled to get free of this guy, and she couldn't." He points to himself and chokes out the words, "But I could. She helped me. I know that her dying saved my life."

Patrick says there's only one thing left he can do for his beloved Sue. He can honor her life by living his well.

DIANE VAN DEREN

If you're looking for amazing people, tap into the world of sports. Athletes are mentally tough and physically strong, and their journeys to the top are often unique and filled with challenges. Hall of Famer Jackie Robinson broke the color barrier in Major League Baseball. Pro surfer Bethany Hamilton excels with only one arm. Comeback kid Dan Jansen won Olympic gold in speed skating after the devastating loss of his sister. A long list of names came my way when I asked for inspirational stories from the NBC sports archives. So many of the candidates were impressive, but one in particular jumped off the page. This against-the-odds athlete couldn't help herself. That's just how Diane Van Deren is; she attacks life with a positive energy that's undeniable and magnetic. Diane's life story is remarkable, and to walk a mile in her shoes is impossible. After all, Diane would never just walk a mile—she'd run at least fifty.

❖

Diane Van Deren is the first brain surgery case of the day at University of Colorado Hospital in Denver. It's February 1997, but for the next three hours, the date and time will be of no concern to Diane; she's under general anesthesia. The neurosurgeon has been instructed to remove as much as possible of his thirty-seven-year-old patient's hippocampus, an area of the brain tucked deep inside the temporal lobes. In Diane's case, the problem area lies within her right hippocampus, just below her right temple.

The surgery is elective for Diane and routine for the highly trained specialists at the hospital. Just before eight A.M., the neurosurgeon begins to slice through the muscle of Diane's scalp. Next, he drills holes in her skull, and then connects the holes using a handheld electric saw. He removes the rectangular piece of bone, about the size of a playing card, and wraps it in a moist towel. Next, the surgeon folds back the lining of Diane's brain. Using a vibrating tube the diameter of a swizzle stick, he knocks loose the damaged brain cells and suctions them out. He then backtracks, closing up each layer. Finally, he reattaches Diane's skull piece using wax and bone chips.

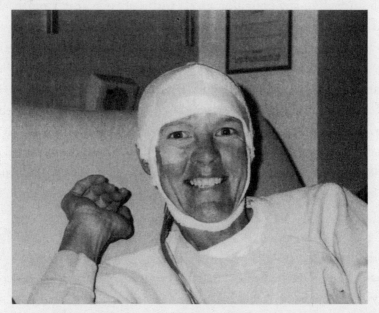

Diane, recovering from February 1997 brain surgery.
(Courtesy of Diane Van Deren)

Why would someone possibly *elect* to have this brain surgery? Routine in the operating room, perhaps; undoubtedly not routine in terms of the decisions most of us make in life. But, clearly, Diane Van Deren is not like most of us.

The trouble began deep inside Diane's brain when she was only sixteen months old. A healthy baby, Diane suddenly developed a high fever. When she started to convulse, her parents and grandmother rushed her to a hospital in Omaha, Nebraska. Packed in ice, Diane's little body quivered for nearly an hour. While doctors spoke with Diane's parents in the hospital room, her grandmother waited just outside. As the doctors came back out into the hallway, her grandmother overheard them saying that Diane's lungs were weak, and her prognosis was questionable.

"One doctor said to the other doctor, 'We don't know if she's going to be a vegetable, we don't know if she's going to survive,'" Diane says. 'She might be better off if she didn't.'"

In 1961, not much was known about the brain and its ability to recover from trauma. What caused the seizure? Was Diane born with an underlying abnormality, or did the high fever cause the seizure? And would the seizures continue? Thankfully, Diane recovered and showed no signs of brain damage. She grew up healthy and happy in Littleton, Colorado, south of Denver.

"I wanted to be a cowgirl," Diane says, thinking back on her active childhood. "I'd be out on the golf course in the private club area whippin' rope around a bale of hay with a plastic bull horn stuck in it. The golfers would drive by in their golf carts and say, 'Hey, Diane!'"

She was notably athletic, the first to be chosen for all the neighborhood games. The boys even asked Diane to play catcher on their baseball team.

She laughs. "So I had to take my pigtails and shove them up into my baseball hat and they had to call me Dan. I knew at a young age I had something different. I remember sitting down with my dad at the breakfast table and saying, 'There's something different about me, Dad. I'm faster and can kick and throw a ball better than the girls. And, Dad, I do it better than the boys. So what's different about me?'"

She says her father told her those were her God-given gifts and that she should use them to her full potential. And boy, did she ever.

Diane competed in every sport she could get her hands and legs on: horseback riding, swimming, track, basketball, and golf. At thirteen, she sold her quarter horse for $500, bought tennis balls and a wooden racket, and developed a new passion: tennis. By the next year, Diane was the Colorado state champion in both tennis and golf. She was also named to the all-state basketball team. Gifted and impassioned, Diane was determined to follow her dream of becoming a professional athlete. In her senior year of high school, Diane set the wheels in motion. She asked several neighbors to help fund her goal to play on the women's pro tennis tour and made arrangements at school to graduate early.

"So here I had two checks in my pocket." Diane smiles. "I wanted to go play pro tennis, I'd already talked to the principal at the school, but I hadn't told my parents yet."

When she did, and pulled out the substantial checks, Diane says her dad's jaw dropped. Game on. With her parents' guarded blessing and steadfast support, she left home and began traveling around the United States and Europe on the women's pro tennis tour. Over the next four years, she would also receive a junior college scholarship to play on a top-ranked tennis team in Odessa, Texas. Diane juggled her time and her teams, playing on both the pro tour and for her college. (She was able to do both by declining any gifts or money on the pro tour.) In her senior year, Diane added yet another challenge to her already full plate: training to compete in Hawaii's Ironman Triathlon, a nonstop competition that requires a 112-mile bike ride, a 2.4-mile swim, and a 26.2-mile run. Diane knew she had the skill set. At twenty two, she'd beaten every woman in a Texas marathon that she'd entered on a whim.

These were extremely active and exciting years for Diane. She was at the top of all her games and thought nothing of the brief out-of-body sensations she began to experience during her twenties.

"It's like a déjà vu feeling," Diane describes. "I'd get this rising feeling in my stomach and I'd get kind of nauseous. It would hit me for thirty seconds, maybe a minute. If I had one, I could still talk to you. On the tour, I'd play through it. And I had that for years."

After graduating with a degree in speech communications from the University of Texas of the Permian Basin and completing her stint on the women's pro tennis tour, Diane came home to Colorado. In the fall of 1982, she invited her mom to join her on a church retreat in the nearby mountains. During their spiritual getaway, Diane and her mom became friends with the woman leading the retreat. They talked of faith and family, and the leader said she felt her son and Diane would hit it off. When they returned home, a blind date was set up with Diane; her parents; the son, Scott; and his parents, the Van Derens. During the dinner, Diane learned that Scott was an avid sailor and was gearing up to sail from California to Hawaii. Intrigued, Diane and Scott had lunch by themselves the following afternoon. The two quickly realized they shared a love of travel and adventure.

"I just really liked her humor, athletic ability, she had traveled, and she was attractive. There was a really good chemistry there," Scott says. "I told my best friend I was going to marry her."

The next day, Scott left for California to prepare for his cross-Pacific adventure. He tracked down the captain of a fifty-seven-foot sailboat, who allowed him to join his five-man crew. Their first stop along the coast was Cabo San Lucas.

"I remember sitting on the beach, two or three weeks after I met Diane, looking at the boat swaying in the water with the moon in the background, and just so excited to be there because I had planned the sailing trip for many years after I graduated from college, and had been looking forward to it, and yet there was something missing. The distinct memory I have was, *This is awesome, but I want someone to share it with.* And I had just met that person, so it was great."

On New Year's day 1983, Scott and four fellow adventurers set sail for Hawaii. Three weeks later, they anchored in Hilo.

"While Scott was in Hawaii, he was checking out the Ironman race course for me, writing notes in the sand," says Diane, "and I was training for the Ironman."

After two and a half months, Scott returned home from his trip. He and Diane continued to date and learn about each other. The two had actually grown up less than three miles apart but attended different schools. Amazingly, their families worshipped in the same church. Four months into their relationship, Scott asked Diane to marry him.

"It didn't seem overly rushed or quick. It just felt like we clicked; it came together at the right time," says Scott. "There was just something really special about the way I connected with Diane."

Engaged and looking ahead to having a family one day, Diane decided to pull out of the Ironman. In August 1983, the twenty-three-year-olds were married. Scott and Diane both worked, he at a Fortune 500 computer company, she at her father's steel company. Always active, Diane continued to run and occasionally competed in local triathlons. The Van Derens began having children three years into their marriage, and by year six, they had a son, a daughter, and a second son on the way.

Several weeks into the third pregnancy, the first sign of a serious medical issue revealed itself. Diane was sitting in a car with her mother, looking at houses for sale.

"We were with a real estate agent looking for a bigger home. We were in the car driving around neighborhoods and I remember my mom saying, 'Honey, can you just grab me a piece of gum out of the glove box?' That's all I remember," Diane says. "I guess my head went back, my body jerked. They thought I was having a heart attack."

At the hospital, doctors were cautious but felt the incident was a fluke. Diane didn't drink, didn't smoke, and had been a pro athlete. They concluded the seizure was hormonal and sent her home. But several months later, during the second trimester of the pregnancy, another episode occurred, at night. This one was big and bad: a grand mal.

"I only remember coming out of it," says Diane. "I was very combative, screaming and yelling. I was fearful, not knowing what was going on."

A grand mal seizure involves a loss of consciousness and violent muscle contractions. Diane's body shook the bed intensely enough to awaken Scott.

"I said to no one, 'Okay, here we go,' just knowing in an instant flash," he says, "that things had probably changed forever."

Scott called 911 while he, in horror, watched a pregnant Diane endure the seizure. It would be the last night that Scott slept soundly for nearly a decade.

"He never slept. Every time I'd gasp or roll, he wanted to make sure I wasn't seizing," Diane says. "Now that's kind of a joke. If he snores, I think, *Eh. Let it go. The poor guy never slept for ten years*. Even now he says, 'Oh, man, when I come to bed and I hear you breathing really hard and you're sleeping so hard, it's so comforting.'"

Both twenty-nine years old, Scott and Diane faced a new normal that stemmed from an old ailment. For so many years, the grand mal seizure that Diane had suffered as a baby seemed like a nonissue. But, in truth, the odd feelings Diane experienced during her twenties were faint warnings. Something dangerous was brewing. During Diane's third pregnancy, her brain's secret life was exposed; the electrical discharges it so boldly unleashed mimicked an internal lightning storm. A medical crisis was now a member of the Van Deren family. Like the world's worst roommates, seizures moved in and began to wreak havoc in their home life. A desperate and lengthy search for answers began, as Scott and Diane raised their three very young children: three-year-old Michael, one-year-old Robin, and newborn Matt.

"What I found so frustrating was, here I had three healthy kids, and I was healthy and vibrant. I felt like I had this incredible life . . ." She pauses. "And these seizures."

Scott and Diane tried their best to structure a life where freedom and a safety net were both well represented.

"I would come home, and she would be pushing two of the kids in the double stroller, and she'd have the third in a backpack, and she's walking the dog." Scott laughs. "The goal, as unrealistic as it was, was to try to have a normal life and to try to do fun things. We lived in a neighborhood where everything was close. We could go sledding a block and a half away, there were tennis courts, there was a pool, Diane's sister lived close by, so we could walk there."

In medical terms, the odd feelings Diane experienced during her twenties were actually something called auras. Auras are warnings; they act as a seizure's calling card.

Hello, I'm about to hijack part of your brain. Could be a small attack, or I might knock you on your ass.

The stealth attacks were maddening. Raising three small children was trying enough; Diane also had the anxiety of wondering whether her own body would suddenly check out.

"That was scary. The fear of the unknown," Diane explains. "We were always at the ready. My confidence was crushed. I always had to think, *What if . . . ?*"

Scott was perpetually on duty as watcher and worrier.

"My reaction was always the same," Scott explains. "If she was thinking about something and became quiet, I thought she was having a seizure. If she was ten minutes late, I was thinking she had a seizure or she's not in a good place, or she crashed the car. You just never knew, and I became very in tune with the sounds and the looks and the tone of voice and her eyes."

Protecting the kids physically and emotionally was a top priority for Scott and Diane. When she went to bed early or missed dinner, Scott would lay out a picnic-style dinner on the basement floor and tell the kids, "Mom just needs to rest." It was more difficult to shield them from the visual horrors.

"It was really disturbing for me to see a seizure, knowing the physical exhaustion and the effort and the negative things that were happening during that seizure," Scott says, "and so we were very protective of the kids about that. I don't think we were entirely successful."

Diane had little control over when a problem flared inside her brain.

"I didn't want my kids to see me having a seizure. As a mom it just sucks. That's what my tears were for. *What am I putting my kids through?*"

Even more stressful: the possible tragic consequences of Diane's having a seizure while she was caring for the children.

"When I took a bath, I'd always let the family know," Diane explains, "and whenever I took the kids swimming, I'd always have to go to the lifeguard and say, 'My kids are fine, but you need to watch me. If my arms aren't going, if I'm not breathing, you gotta come get me.'"

They eventually hired a nanny to help Diane but still wanted to arm the kids with preventative measures.

"My kids at a very young age had to learn how to drive a car, because if Mom seized in the car, they would have to know how to take over," Diane says. "We lived on a ranch with a John Deere tractor, and we'd take the kids out and teach them to steer. Grandma and Grandpa would take them out in golf carts, too."

Diane always drove in the right lane so she could easily pull over to the side of the road if she experienced an aura. Driving became a source of tension for the Van Derens, as Diane battled for normalcy and Scott managed reality. They ultimately hired a driver.

"If Diane says, 'I feel okay, I can drive,' she is an adult and she can make that decision. But if she's driving *our* children, and I think her eyes are sunken and I don't think she looks quite right in the morning, then I have an opinion about that."

Determined to gain more control over Diane's seizures and their family life, the couple was constantly on the hunt for effective doctors and drugs. Prescribed medications were ineffective. Diane was either allergic to the meds or suffered from their side effects. Her seizures raged weekly.

"Our life revolved around what Diane needed. The parts of that Diane was aware of," Scott says, "she really resented and really did not like. She was very embarrassed when she had a seizure. She didn't want the attention, she didn't want to be a bother, she wanted to be self-reliant, and she didn't want help from other people. She resented not the family, but having to be in that situation, or to have other people see her have a seizure or not be her normal fun-loving self."

After repeated visits to various doctors over the years, Diane was diagnosed with epilepsy—basically, another word for the condition of someone who suffers from recurrent seizures.

"I didn't know how to spell it, didn't know what it was, didn't know what it meant," Scott says. "It was, at that time, a really big word with a very negative connotation."

Scott and Diane armed themselves with as much information as they could about epilepsy. Scott scoured the Internet, read books, and reached out to the area Epilepsy Foundation for guidance. They were both exhausted, drained from the combination of ordinary and extraordinary challenges. Scott was juggling his many roles: father, husband, businessman, patient advocate, and fill-in mom.

"It's like if your toilet's overflowing, you gotta do what you gotta do. I was simply reacting over the years. When's the next doctor's appointment? How's Diane doing today? What needs to get done?" he says. "Yeah, there were some times when you just became exhausted, but it was pretty much, what needs to happen today and what are we gonna do about it?"

The daily uncertainty dominated the mood and focus of the entire family. No one meant to lay out an invisible layer of eggshells, but sidestepping it was nearly impossible in the Van Deren house.

"I remember the talks with the kids. I remember the, 'Mommy, are you gonna get better?' The kids didn't want to upset me or stress Mommy out because they thought if Mommy had a seizure it was their fault." The limitations for Diane created by the seizures were extremely difficult for her to accept. As an athlete and active mom, she despised the intrusion of epilepsy.

"Diane did not take it seriously enough," Scott says. "I had multiple differences of opinion and discussions with her. 'No, honey, you didn't eat something bad yesterday, this is related to your seizures.' 'Denial' might be too strong of a word. She only knew and understood what was happening in her head and she thought that was normal. For us, it was just this ever-present fog of not quite understanding everything that was happening and not knowing the way out."

Diane also hated taking medications, another source of tension between her and Scott.

"Diane would get on effective meds and stop having seizures, and say, 'Hey, look. I'm not having seizures. I don't need the meds anymore.' And then have a seizure. That happened probably three different times."

Managing the unpredictable was complicated. Everyone wanted to protect Diane; Diane wanted to live a full life.

"Her dad would come over to the house," Scott says, "and Diane would be working in the garden and it would be hot out, and her dad would say, 'Diane, you can't work in the garden! You have to stop or you'll have a seizure.' That was the exact opposite of what Diane wanted to do, so she'd stop, and her dad would leave, and she'd go back out into the garden and work."

The dilemma was that Diane's decisions and their resulting consequences affected everyone. A seizure was the lead domino in a cascading series of kid shuffling and task reorganization.

"The tough time was not even the day of the seizure, especially if she had a grand mal seizure; it was the day after," Scott explains. "The recovery from the seizure would just lay her out."

During a grand mal seizure, the entire brain is engaged, as well as the body's muscles, which strain and contract. In an effort to stop the seizure, the brain does too good of a job, shutting down everything from emotions to memory. While the seizure itself lasts for perhaps a minute, the brain's busy work of shutting down and rebooting every system can continue for hours.

"When you come out of it," Diane describes, "you feel like you've been hit by a truck."

In 1995, by chance, Diane discovered a possible strategy for eluding a seizure. She was walking the family's golden Labrador retriever about two miles from home. Suddenly, she felt the onset of an aura.

"I started running home. I just thought, *I gotta get home to a safe spot*. And when I got home, I realized I didn't seize. And I thought, *Wow!*"

From that day forward, Diane used running as the most powerful weapon against her very worthy and wily opponent, epilepsy.

"My thought was, *I'm gonna beat it. I'm gonna beat this SOB.*"

Diane's running shoes were never far from reach. When an aura bloomed, she'd strap on her shoes and hit the trail leading to the Pike National Forest, six miles from her backyard. Her goal was to run as long as it took to block the seizure, sometimes a two- or three-hour outing.

"That's where my love for long-distance running came from. I'd run for hours. The fear of the seizure was just gone. It was euphoric. It was my safe spot. It was heaven."

The strategy worked often, but circumstances didn't always allow for an escape. The reality was, Diane frequently seized at inopportune moments: during a work dinner for Scott, in a crowded movie theater, in front of hundreds of spectators while coaching her daughter's basketball team. Regrettably, the auras began to offer Diane shorter and shorter warnings. Chronic seizures, small and large, for more than fifteen years, created medical mayhem in her brain.

The Van Derens were running out of options. Medications and multiple doctors were not providing solutions.

"I had one doctor who told me, 'You'll never drive, you'll never swim alone, you'll never beat epilepsy, here's your prescription,'" she says. "And I looked him in the eye and I said, 'You son of a bitch.' And I just walked out. I kept going and going until I found a doctor that let me be me."

She found him in 1996. The executive director of the Epilepsy Foundation of Colorado referred Diane and Scott to Dr. Mark Spitz, a neurologist at the University of Colorado. Interestingly, Diane was not a unique case. Spitz says about a third of epilepsy patients continue to have seizures even though they are taking proven epilepsy medications.

"She was very frustrated," recalls Spitz. "If you take her as an individual, what was especially hard for her was that she had been a very high-functioning person. She was an outstanding athlete in high school and college, and with all of her seizures, she was afraid to go out of the house. She couldn't drive, and to quote her, she had three kids, and her kids were mothering her; she couldn't mother her own children."

Diane shared with Spitz that running was the only way she could partially control her seizures. While Spitz had seen other patients who'd developed a strategy to abort their seizures—like a firefighter who would grab his shaky right wrist with his stable left hand when a tremor began—he had never known someone to use running as a suppression tool. He calls the concept a real medical phenomenon, not just Diane's imagination. Spitz explains that when brain cells are restful (for instance, when you are eating at a quiet restaurant or watching a movie), they are more apt to accept the invasion of abnormal electrical activity that sparks a seizure.

"In contrast, I think what was happening with Diane when she was running," Spitz says, "is that she would get in a specific mindset where the cells the seizure might normally spread into instead wouldn't accept that abnormal activity. The seizure would start, but it would fizzle out. It wouldn't go anywhere."

The first move for Dr. Spitz was to put Diane through a series of neuropsychiatric tests to assess her memory and brain function. Not surprisingly, based on Diane's extensive history of seizures, the results indicated she suffered from short-term memory loss and problems with directional aptitude.

"The part of her brain that was abnormal to begin with, that her seizures emanated from, has two main jobs: one is short-term memory, the other is processing information with regards to its emotional content," he says. "The seizures that she'd had over the years further injured her brain, and her brain wasn't normal because of that."

Spitz next ordered an MRI for Diane. The results were telling. Images revealed scarring of her right hippocampus. The doctor saw hardening and shrinkage of cells in a very isolated area.

"The next step was that I had this hypothesis that her seizures were coming from a relatively regionalized region of her brain, and that it was a region of her brain that we could safely remove surgically, and hopefully stop her seizures and not leave her with a significant neurological deficit."

In June 1996, the doctor began a procedure considered standard in major medical centers around the country. He admitted Diane to Denver's University Hospital so she could have several seizures in a controlled setting. Technicians wired up the outside of her head with electrodes so experts could monitor her brain's electrical data during the seizures. Diane would also be videotaped seizing, since specific body movements also indicate the epicenter of a seizure.

"What I'm interested in as an epileptologist, specifically for this type of surgery, is not how big and bad the seizures are, but anatomically where they start," Spitz explains, "because where they start is the key to the possibility of doing surgery."

Diane hoped fervently for a seizure to occur while she was hooked up in the hospital. It did. When she felt the aura come on, she willed her body not to fight it, but instead to let it flow, knowing intense pain would follow. Diane's brain generated multiple seizures during her four-day stay, one a grand mal. Diane says when she came out of it, she heard Dr. Spitz cheering.

"He was like, 'Yeah! We got it! We got it!'"

Data revealed where in the brain Diane's seizures were originating.

"It was the sweetest spot," says Spitz. "If I could have put it anywhere in her brain, that's where I would have put it."

Here's where we revisit the question posed at the beginning of Diane's story: Why would someone possibly *elect* to have brain surgery? The reality for Diane was, the risks of having surgery (a blind spot in her vision, a 3 percent chance of a stroke, an even lesser chance of dying) were smaller than the risk of *not* having surgery. Diane could either lose a golf-ball-sized chunk of her brain or, very probably, lose her life.

"She would have continued to have seizures, and there are good studies that tell us that continued seizures of her type would have caused her memory and other brain functions to continue to deteriorate further," says Spitz. "The other thing is death. If you look at good statistics, the chance of dying for her as a direct result of a seizure after ten years was one in ten."

Diane was a mother of three, a wife, a gifted athlete, and a fighter. She'd finally found in surgery the sword she needed to slay the beast once and for all.

"Oh, slam dunk," Diane says. "I didn't have any hesitation. I really and truly felt like I was at such a risk of dying at that point. You can call it radical brain surgery, but what was really radical were the three to five seizures a week. I couldn't get it fast enough."

Diane's eagerness was also driven by a stark black and white video image. Back when she was lying in bed at University Hospital, hooked up to electrodes, exhausted from a grand mal seizure, Diane asked Dr. Spitz to show her the videotape they rolled to capture her movements.

"I had no idea. I'd never seen anyone have a seizure," Diane says, shaking her head. "And, whew. Wow. That's the first time I understood why my family lived in fear. I understood why my son developed anxiety in class. My oldest would sit there in his coat all day like, *Is my mom okay?* When I saw that tape, it was the piece of the puzzle that was missing. I was always comforting everyone, 'Mom's fine, don't worry.' But then when I saw what I looked like, I could be more empathetic. I had chunked off a piece of my tongue. I have blood running down the side of my face. You can hear me on the tape just, 'huh, huh, huh' [rapid breathing sounds]. I have all this blood going down the back of my throat. I'm gurgling, I'm exhausted, I'm blue. I'm just trashed. And as I come to, I'm disoriented. I don't know who's who. And I have a massive headache."

The time had come. On February 20, 1997, Diane celebrated her thirty-seventh birthday. Several days later, the night before her surgery, she had one last grand mal seizure. Diane was now just hours away from a potentially life-changing operation.

"I remember being in the operating room and I was joking around," Diane says, "and then I turned to see all this equipment on a table and I said, 'Okay, time to put me to sleep.'"

In the waiting room, Scott was joined by Diane's mother, his brother, and his parents. Diane's father had died four years earlier. The kids, now eleven, nine, and eight, stayed home with the nanny. Scott slipped away to visit the chapel downstairs.

"I remember saying a prayer in the chapel that day"—his voice cracks—"about Diane being God's precious lamb and not knowing the outcome. It was beyond my control."

The surgery, described at the start of this story, went smoothly. In terms of her prognosis, if Diane could live one year without having a seizure, she would most likely never have another. There would be one post-op complication: a blind spot that affects Diane's upper-right peripheral vision. The other complication was accidental, caused by Diane herself. Her shunt, a tube that drains excess spinal fluid from the brain to another part of the body, was sticking out of Diane's head bandage as she lay in the intensive care unit.

"When I came around I was quite combative, and I grabbed that shunt and dislodged it. When I grabbed the shunt, the fluid had nowhere to go," she says, "and I was lying there in the most excruciating pain. I was kicking and dropping F bombs. But I didn't know. I was in La La Land. I thought everyone was hurting me. I even pulled out my IVs and took off down the hallway. They eventually strapped me down. I was in such pain."

After eight days in the hospital, Diane returned home. She focused on recovery and regaining the fifteen pounds she'd lost post-op. The Van Derens had hired a nanny a month before the surgery to familiarize her with the family; she stepped in to help with the kids when Diane went in for the operation. Back in her own bed and relatively rested, Diane soon began to feel the itch to run, her "medicine" for so many years. (She does *not* recommend this idea for anyone else.)

"After a few weeks, I was at the house and I could hop. Just three steps," admits Diane. "And I thought, *Hot damn! If I can hop, I can run!* I remember tying my shoe and holding my head. The pressure was awful, but I just wanted to get on that mountain. I knew my running was my healing."

The physical challenges ahead were huge for Diane, but she also faced a significant emotional hurdle. Dr. Spitz says he broaches the topic with all of his brain injury patients before they undergo surgery.

"I tell everybody: the hardest thing about what you're going to go through is nothing medical. What you're going to have to do with your family and friends is to figure out where you fit in this world when your life is not dominated by epilepsy. Are you going to go to school? Are you going to get a new job? What are you going to do?" Spitz explains, "These people are often very disabled psychosocially. They're overprotected by family and friends, and we're gonna take that all away from them."

The answers to those questions for Diane lay, literally, at her feet. She hit the ground running, euphoric about the new health and life she'd been given through surgery. Only time would determine if her seizures were gone for good, but Diane felt relieved and hopeful. The "What are you going to do?" concern did not apply to her.

"Diane did not have that problem," Scott says emphatically.

The real problem was finding balance with this new normal. The family was eager to partake in the long-awaited freedom from worry, but was it smart, for instance, to ride horses as a family? Diane's answer was always yes, full speed ahead.

"It was an awkward time," Scott explains. "Everybody was so joyful that she got through surgery, but we'd been so focused on ending the seizures that we never thought about what she would do after surgery. Everybody just wanted her to be really careful. There were two sides to it. What were we going to do with this new health? The family was trying to pull back a bit and she wanted to absolutely surge forward."

Diane thrived, tackling the mountain trails, increasing her distances. Scott, an outdoorsman himself, understood the immense pleasure Diane gained from nature and exercise and supported her efforts.

In the summer of 2002, Diane decided to enter a fifty-mile trail run, an ultramarathon, in Winter Park, Colorado, about an hour northwest of their home in Sedalia. An ultramarathon is defined as any race longer than the approximately 26.2 miles of a traditional marathon. Ultra runners tackle distances anywhere from fifty to one hundred and even four hundred and thirty miles along trails that can span from a sandy beach to a high-altitude mountaintop. They may run for days on end in brutal weather conditions with no sleep and no aid station for forty miles. And there's no prize money at the finish line. The names of the races alone would make even the fittest of athletes run the other way: the HURT 100, the Yukon Arctic Ultra 300, the Canadian Death Race.

Diane had never run an ultramarathon and had been simply enjoying the freedom of twenty-mile local trail runs by herself. Now she was ready to dig deeper. Scott supported her decision and joined her at the start and finish of her first fifty-mile race. The only runner Diane met that day was Richard Neslund. Twenty runners had signed up, but nearly all of them chose at the last minute to run elsewhere. Richard and Diane were the only ultramarathoners to run the course, which included a trip along the western slope of the Continental Divide in the central Rocky Mountains.

Although he's been running marathons for twenty years, Richard doesn't consider himself anything other than an "old fart" who won't share his age and runs only to decompress. When he met Diane the day of the fifty-mile race, he was surprised to hear that she'd never run an ultra. Less than ten miles into the race, Diane dropped a bombshell. She informed Richard that she had a brain injury, and although she hadn't had a seizure in five years, there was a possibility she could have one at any time.

"As soon as she said it," Richard recalls, "all I could remember with my primitive medical knowledge was, *Okay, a seizure. You're supposed to have a pencil and put it between your teeth. What do I do? I have no idea what to do.*"

Diane laughs. "I'll never forget the look on his face! Richard is very type A, very planned out. The poor guy!"

Unable to keep Diane's pace, Richard eventually faded back and Diane found herself alone on the trail.

"Hey," Diane jokes, "I knew if I seized he'd find me eventually."

Diane finished the fifty miles five hours ahead of Richard. The two have remained friends ever since.

"After I finished that event," says Diane, "Richard sent me a notebook about how to train, what hyponatremia is—a full notebook on ultra running. What a friend."

While supportive, Scott was somewhat unclear on this new direction Diane was taking with her running.

"We got through that first one and I thought it might just go away," he admits. "Turned out not to be the case."

Diane set her sights on one hundred miles. "I get bored easily," she says with a laugh.

She signed up for the Leadville Trail 100, a high-altitude challenge in the former silver-mining town of Leadville, Colorado, elevation ten thousand feet. The race begins at three thirty A.M. and there is always an August mix of snow and rain. Hungry for a challenge, Diane was excited to test her body and mind. Scott was disturbed.

"Clearly it was not wise in my mind. It was the worst possible race conditions," he reasons. "It was physical exertion and sleep deprivation.

The way she made herself have a seizure in the hospital was riding her stationary bike and sleep deprivation. So, you're out of the hospital and have this newfound health that we have all suffered mightily for over the years, gladly, to get you to a place where you're healthy, and I understand you love to run, but now you want to do this?"

Diane saw it differently, through the lens of a person who'd been a prisoner of epilepsy for a decade.

"For ten years I lived, *What if, what if?* There were still no guarantees, but I had a new confidence. Everyone had to adjust. Scott was always so nurturing—protecting, protecting. And the kids, too. And then you enter this world where you're not seizing anymore and they have to let go of those feelings. It's huge. When I ran my first one hundred, everybody was a wreck."

Diane never seized, but at seventy miles, she twisted her knee on the rugged terrain. She managed to hobble along for several miles.

"It was very late at night at the aid station and she was hurt," says Scott. "I remember thinking, *If she doesn't finish, then she's gonna come back and do it again.* I really wanted her to finish."

But at mile seventy-two, Diane dropped out of the race. But not for good.

"That kind of gave me a flavor of what a one hundred would be like," says Diane. "I learned from that and it made me hungrier."

She began a rigorous training program that included a one-hundred-miles-per-week running schedule loaded with high-altitude training and consecutive twenty-five-mile runs.

In June 2003, Diane completed the Bighorn Trail 100 Mile Run in Wyoming. She was the sixth woman to cross the finish line, in just under thirty-two hours.

"I really thought that was it," Diane says. "Honestly, in my heart I thought, *I didn't seize, I proved a bunch of doctors wrong, and I just placed in one of the top four hardest races in the country.*"

But several days later, the phone rang. Her dear friend who headed up the Epilepsy Foundation of Colorado called to ask if Diane would speak to a group of thirty grade-schoolers at a camp for kids with severe epilepsy. Still banged up from the race, Diane agreed to drive the seventy miles to Granby. At the camp, Diane sat in a circle with the children and played her guitar. She encouraged the group to live life to the fullest.

"I told them, 'If you want to drive a car, you go out to the country and sit on someone's lap,'" Diane says. "'If you want to swim in the ocean, just have someone with you. If you want to parachute, you tether to someone. There's nothing you can't do having epilepsy. You just have to approach it differently and think smart.'"

Diane says the kids were having seizures even as she spoke with them. Then, a question.

"One girl said, 'Diane, would you run your next hundred-mile race for me? I have epilepsy and I have cerebral palsy and I can't run. Will you do that for me?'" Diane recalls. "And then all the other kids started asking, 'Yeah! Would you run for us?' They asked me to let the world know they were normal, that there's nothing different about them. I looked around and thought, *Wow. I've been given a gift. This isn't my life anymore.*"

Thus began a very busy eight years for Diane. And the very tricky portioning of her time pie—the training slice versus the family slice.

"Once I got through the seizures and knew I wasn't going to have any, I got kind of selfish, sure," Diane admits. "In my heart there was a part of me that was like, *We've raised the kids, I've got a wonderful husband,* but I couldn't do the things I wanted to do because I always had to think, *What if . . . ?* That's when I got confident, and I just cut loose. I just kind of felt like, *Okay, this is my time.* I started doing well in my running and I'd been a pro athlete before and I knew what it took, and I started excelling. And that took over my time."

Scott saw clearly that Diane had found a second life as an accomplished athlete. It now made the best sense to join in the adventure.

Family vacations became incorporated into many of Diane's exciting events. "I took the kids, we went to the start, and then the kids and I went and hiked a fourteener [a mountain that exceeds fourteen thousand feet above mean sea level], and then we went back for the finish," Scott explains. "One of the kids would cross the finish line with Diane, and so we tried to make it a family event."

That November, Diane entered and came in first in the women's division, and second overall, in the San Diego 100 Mile Endurance Run. Soon after, she really cut loose. In 2004, Diane competed in eight ultras, from the mountain trails of Colorado, to the lush wilderness of Hawaii, to the frozen rivers of Alaska, to France's majestic Mont Blanc. She even tackled the Hardrock 100 in Silverton, Colorado, among the hardest hundred-mile trail races in the world. Runners navigate steep climbs and descents, snowpacks, river crossings, and boulder fields. Of the 150 runners who compete, only about half finish the race within the allotted forty-eight hours. Scott served as a member of Diane's crew team for many of the ultras she tackled.

The tremendously taxing race schedule eventually began to reveal some areas in Diane's life that needed work. She knew what she had gained from the surgery, but there was never any exploration of what she'd lost to the many years of chronic seizure damage.

"People see me excel athletically, and then when I see someone and I don't remember who they are, or I lose my sense of direction just a couple blocks away from where I need to be," Diane says, "there is a disconnect—and with my family, too. My kids have grown up with it, but there's been a lot of hurt and frustration. Even with my mother, who I love dearly. She'll say, 'How can you be doing all this, and then forget this?' And that is what just"—she sighs—"makes me cry, because you don't mean to hurt."

Diane turned to a neuropsychologist at Craig Hospital in Englewood, Colorado, a facility renowned for its work with patients recovering from brain and spinal cord injuries. The doctor put Diane through a series of tests to identify her neurological deficits. The results were revealing.

"'How do you function?'" Diane says the doctor asked her. "'How do you function on a daily basis?' And that blew me away."

Diane had been navigating her personal and professional life without the tools she needed as a brain-injury victim. She had no short-term memory, had no sense of direction, had difficulty managing emotional content, and was easily prone to mental fatigue.

"I'll never forget that, because when I left that office I was crying. I thought, *No wonder! No wonder my kids were hurt. No wonder I couldn't remember.*"

Now enlightened, Diane was eager for the doctor's guidance on how to thrive within the constraints of her brain damage.

"He started to give me the tools. 'This is why you get lost, this is how you have to pack, this is why when you arrive for a race you can't be worrying about what you need—write it on your bag, write it on your hand.' Now I always have a laminated note down my running bra because I can't afford to forget anything."

Advance preparation is key. Before a big race, Diane declares the Van Derens' dining room table off-limits. Meat and potatoes are replaced by headlamps and expedition boots.

"I start laying stuff out weeks before my event because I have to visualize the route and what I'll need, because I can't read a map or GPS well." Diane laughs. "Everyone knows not to follow me. North Face always says I'm the barometer for how well a race is marked. If I don't get lost, nobody can complain about getting lost on the course."

The collaboration with the doctor (whom Diane has asked not be identified due to his confidential work with other professional athletes) continues to be a vital component of her racing career.

"People ask me, 'What's the hardest part of an event?' and I say, 'Packing! Getting to the airport! Finding my gate!'" She laughs. "How many times have I heard over the speakers, 'Diane Van Deren, your passport is back at the security station. Diane Van Deren, we're waiting for you at gate twelve.' It's all harder than the race. When I get to the start of a race, I just go. I don't worry about anything, and that to me is my medicine. I just listen to the wind and my breath, and my brain just goes, *Oh, baby, this is it*."

The neuropsychologist also helped stock Diane's tool kit for her personal life. He suggested that her family should offer up more cues and reminders throughout the day.

"'Mom, we have to leave in thirty minutes,'" Diane mimics, "where normally, Mom wouldn't be anywhere close to being ready, or Mom would be late because of my problems with time. That's why I burn stuff all the time. I put something in the oven, then go outside to fill up the horse tank or something, and come in and, boom! Burnt."

The doctor also explained that mental fatigue is a significant issue for a brain-injury victim. Grouchy behavior is the brain's way of signaling, *I'm done for today*.

"I'd be go, go, go all day with the kids and coaching and I'd come home and I'd say to Scott, 'Why am I so irritable? Why am I so grumpy?' I remember saying that to him for years. And the kids would see it. They'd see Mom being short, and that wasn't me."

Diane's more than seven years of therapy with the neuropsychologist have helped the Van Derens better understand her limitations. Family calendars, dozens of sticky notes, and backups to the backup reminders are vital.

"If I don't see it I'll forget about it. I have it here," Diane says, pointing to a large calendar, "then I have another note on my fridge in case the calendar gets a little overwhelming for my head, and then I have another reminder on my phone alarm."

When her kids' birthdays roll around, she places notes throughout the house and in the car to remember to call. Simply recognizing that she needs help at times was an essential tip for Diane from the doctor.

"He told me I shouldn't be afraid when I see somebody to tell them, 'I have a brain injury; I need some help.' I never used to say that."

Diane jokes about the days when she didn't write things down and, as a result, would ask a dozen people for directions in a city she'd traveled to for a speaking engagement.

"When I was in Chattanooga, a guy in the audience raised his hand and said, 'Do you remember me? I'm the guy on the bike you asked for directions!'" She laughs, "I'd get to know half the city when I'd go running before a speech in town."

The same year Diane began working with the neuropsychologist at Craig Hospital, she met Barb Page, who is now one of her dearest friends.

"When I look at her," says Barb, "it's like you see molecules just bouncing off each other. That's how I see Diane—her brain, her muscles, her being. It's just hard for her to sit down and relax, ever. She is in constant motion in her head and in her heart and in her body."

Barb was working in 2004 as the executive director of the Craig Hospital Foundation. She met Diane when they both were involved in coordinating a philanthropic tour of the hospital. An early bond developed between the two because of Barb's familiarity with the challenges of traumatic brain injuries.

"She wants to believe she's capable of doing more than she can do," says Barb, "and she'll beat up on herself. And I'll say, 'Diane, you've lost part of your brain. You can't compensate for everything.'"

Over the years, Barb has become Diane's sounding board, and also a voice of reason. At seventy-two, Barb says she can offer Diane motherly advice.

"I often say, 'When you go to X, Y, Z city, you are not to rent a car but instead take a taxi.' It's things a mother would do in many ways, but she usually listens to me."

Usually, but not always. Barb says the same steely determination that makes Diane an elite athlete can also get her into trouble.

"She flew to Atlanta to be part of a meeting seventy miles away, and I said, 'Diane, you cannot get in a car and make that drive by yourself.' Well, her hardheadedness came into play and she did it. And it took her an hour and a half to find a highway that's ten minutes from the airport."

Diane admits, "She knows me much better that way than I probably know myself. With a brain injury, we can be impulsive and we can be . . ." She snaps her fingers twice, signaling urgency. "She helps me pause and think, *Y'know, you're right*. And the beauty of the friendship is I don't have to hide anything; she understands. I can be more open and share things with her."

In 2005, the trail miles began to increase exponentially for Diane. She'd also signed on with the North Face as one of the company's sponsored endurance athletes and speakers. The running world knew nothing of Diane's struggles with brain damage, not even the North Face. When she first began competing, Diane tucked a seizure pill wrapped in foil inside her hydration pack, just in case.

"I didn't want to be treated differently," Diane says. "I didn't want to be judged. I didn't want to incite fear in a race director. I knew I was responsible for me. I wanted to prove myself as an athlete."

But in late 2005, the death of a little boy brought Diane's personal story to life.

She was working with a foundation in Breckenridge, Colorado, that raised money for adults and children with disabilities. At a winter fund-raiser, Diane was approached by a family after she delivered the event's keynote speech. The Nelsons told Diane that their six-year-old son suffered from seizures and that he was a possible candidate for the brain surgery that had helped Diane.

"I met Hunter," Diane says, "and he was so precious. I tried to tell his parents what it felt like for him to have seizures, and I encouraged them to have the surgery. They told me they were good friends with Garth Brooks."

The country music superstar had arranged to fly Hunter to a facility where he'd be put through the same electroencephalogram test that Diane had undergone to determine the focal point of his seizures. The surgery could change his life, as it had hers. But on the day of the scheduled flight, there was heartbreaking news.

"I got the phone call that Hunter had died," Diane says softly, "and that's the morning I was driving up to the Teva Mountain Games in Vail, trying to hold it together."

The night before the plane was to pick him up, Hunter suffered a seizure and suffocated in his sleep. Devastated, Diane began to feel a plan unfolding in her mind. Here she was, surrounded by the top athletes in the world, at a well-known annual event covered by the mainstream media, sponsored by a global company. Now was the time. This was the way to honor the kids at camp years earlier who'd asked Diane to tell the world they were just like everybody else. The plan came together when Diane's name was announced as Female Runner of the Year.

"I was standing up there onstage holding this trophy," Diane describes, "and that's when I shared. I just pictured Hunter and it was just time. A little boy had just lost his life to a seizure and that's when I stood onstage and said, 'I want to dedicate this trophy to little Hunter Nelson.' I said, 'Ten years ago today I couldn't even take a bath alone, because if I had a seizure I could drown. I'm here now today, running all the hardest races in the world, because of surgery. I'm here and Hunter isn't.'"

Now the world knew. This elite athlete was the incredible woman she was despite the challenges she'd been dealt. Her close friend Richard, whom she told of her seizures that very first ultra race, defines her not as an ultra runner, but rather as an ultra lifer. He says adversity fuels Diane's passion for excellence.

"Many of us look at things and we might have an inner conversation about why we want to achieve that thing, but then we also have a whole committee of voices in there about why we can't achieve it. All the excuses kick in: *Oh, I haven't trained, I don't have the right equipment, I don't have the time,* or *Poor me, I have a foot injury,*" says Richard. "But with Diane, she has plenty of reasons. She could make excuses, but she never uses them. Instead, she says, 'Okay, this is what happened to me, I'm gonna succeed here, even though I've been given an extra challenge.' She leverages what other people may call a handicap in a way that gives her strength. There's a flame inside her that won't go out."

In addition to five other ultramarathons in 2005, Diane decided to compete in her longest race yet: the Iditarod Trail Invitational. You've probably heard of the Iditarod or have watched teams of sled dogs pull their mushers across the endless, barren miles of Alaska. The race Diane signed up for didn't allow dog power. For the Iditarod Trail Invitational, Diane had to pull her own sled, packed with forty pounds of supplies and survival gear. The course spanned 350 miles through frozen tundra. Temperatures reached 60 degrees below zero, and the winter daylight was brief. When Diane told Scott she was going, he was angry. They had not discussed her decision as a couple. He felt a maddening mix of being disrespected and being afraid for his wife.

"That was a tough day. It was winter and we live four point eight miles from Sedalia," says Scott. "I remember putting on full Gore-Tex and gloves and a hat and I walked to and from Sedalia in the middle of the night. I think I came home at three thirty in the morning. I just couldn't process it."

Scott was conflicted. He loved that Diane followed her heart, but he wanted her to take her common sense with her. He'd joined her often enough during races to know that she had fantastic instincts and an innate ability to make solid decisions under pressure. It was the things Scott couldn't control, like Mother Nature, that scared him. Once he accepted the fact that Diane was going, he began to research the Iditarod Trail Invitational. He found the controllable risks to be generally minimal. There would be a large support team and there would always be other competitors along the route with Diane. Scott was on board.

2005 Iditarod Trail Invitational. (Credit: Whit Richardson Photography)

Diane, serving as musher and dog, began the long haul of pulling a sled across 350 miles of unforgiving tundra. She covered fifty miles each day, trying to complete the race in seven days while battling hurricane-force winds and hostile wildlife.

"The moose are huge in Alaska, and that's the first time I've ever had to sign a waiver that if a moose kicked me, the race people were not liable." Diane chuckles. "And I thought, *A moose? C'mon.* But if you run across a moose, they'll stomp you, they'll attack you, they'll kill you. They're very aggressive animals."

Sure enough, it was a moose that took Diane out of the race. Not the animal itself, but the deep hole left behind by a moose as it walked through the snow. While navigating a steep embankment in the dark, wearing a headlamp, Diane accidentally stepped into a moose hole. The weight of her sled yanked her body backward, causing a groin pull. The next aid station was eighty miles away, so Diane was forced to painstakingly drag her strained leg with one hand and her sled with the other. When she finally hobbled into the aid station, which consisted of a tarp, she tried to rest her leg. Her ankle, which she would learn later was stress fractured, was so swollen she couldn't cram it back into her boot. Diane was forced to pull out of the race at 260 miles.

"That's when I said, 'Screw it. If I'm gonna do this again, I'm gonna do something harder, colder, and farther.'"

That would be the Yukon Arctic Ultra 300, billed as the world's coldest and toughest ultra. Scott was apprehensive but once again took a deep breath.

"If you can see her eyes light up when she talks about the Yukon and the welcoming people and the crisp bitter cold and the sun," he says with a lilt in his voice, "and the way the stars reflect on the snow . . . I understand the appeal of all that. It just brings her alive. I just . . . worry about her."

Diane's mother has also struggled with the adventurous spirit of her daughter. Scott says he came up with an analogy for her mom that also comforts him. He pictures an aviator who blazed her trail in the sky.

"I can just see the scarf blowing back in the wind and her looking out of the plane. Amelia Earhart was born to fly. She probably didn't stay home and sew socks or make beef stew a lot, and we wouldn't expect her to. Clearly, Diane has carved out this niche that she was intended to be in: inspiring other people; using her ability; being connected to the North Face, which gives her this chance to represent a company in a positive way and influence young girls about things that they can do; and she relates to people about overcoming obstacles. So, I struggle sometimes and get frustrated when I don't get enough Diane time, and yet I'm part of something that's even bigger." He adds, jokingly, "But sometimes, I would like to come home and have beef stew for dinner."

TEN YEARS LATER

In 2007, a decade after her brain surgery, Diane was thriving. The operation had given her the freedom from worry and harm she'd so desperately wanted for herself and her family. That year, Diane spoke to three different groups about hope for beating epilepsy and how to manage the inevitable challenges of life. On the ultramarathon circuit, Diane's feet did the talking. She ran seven grueling races, besting her former finish time in the Hardrock 100 by three hours.

The following year, Diane headed north for the "harder, colder, and farther" race she sought. In February 2008, Diane traveled to the Canadian Yukon, just below the Arctic Circle, to compete in the Yukon Arctic Ultra 300. She once again pulled a sled, this time laden with fifty pounds of supplies, in merciless fifty-degrees-below-zero temperatures. Diane applied all she'd learned during the Iditarod Trail Invitational to avoid frostbite and hypothermia. At one point in the race, her water bottles froze solid, leaving her with no hydration for twenty miles. She faced seventy-mile-per-hour winds that drove her to her knees when she reached the Yukon River. In the bluster, she lost track of the trail, but eventually rediscovered it after a four-hour detour. One of her navigational tools was to leave behind pieces of colored ribbon that she carried in her first aid kit.

"Let's just say I got lost, and I'd go along on a trail and not see another mile marker. I could come back and tear off a piece of that pink ribbon and put it on top of the snow with a stick or big piece of ice on top, then I'd know when I came back that I'd already been that way; go this way instead."

Nearly eight days later, she was the first racer to cross the finish line. Diane had beaten the Arctic and every one of her thirteen competitors from all over the world.

"I love pressure," says Diane. "I do really well under pressure because pressure feeds me and challenges me."

The following winter, just when Diane thought she had seen the last of the Arctic, race organizers added an additional 130 miles to the event she had won. Diane couldn't resist the new challenge. She signed up for the 2009 Yukon Arctic Ultra 430. Scott, again, processed the mental gymnastics of supporting the pro athlete but missing his wife.

"How can I not limit you," he explains, "but how can we do things together when we're not doing things together?"

He again researched the most effective ways to keep track of Diane. He would follow her progress through a satellite tracker and use the Internet to keep abreast of weather conditions. He knew she would be armed with the experience gained from completing the Yukon 300.

The course started in Whitehorse, Yukon; traversed the Yukon and Takhini Rivers; and ended in Dawson City, Yukon. Facing subzero winds and just seven hours of daylight, competitors had thirteen days to travel 430 miles. Once again, Diane towed a sled packed with forty-five pounds of supplies. Her small stove was crucial for melting snow into drinking water and for cooking meals that provided Diane the ten thousand calories a day she burned. Nuts, cheese, chocolate, peanut butter—foods with a high fat content were essentials. Diane relied heavily on sliced-up mini loaves of nutrient-packed bread a German baker made for her in his Yukon bakery. He also baked her dense, wholesome fruitcake that didn't freeze (Diane doesn't know why). Like a chipmunk, she jammed food into her ski mask and ate it in intervals; the strategy was to avoid having to take her gloves off frequently to grab calories. Racing the clock, Diane napped, at most, three hours each day. She traveled a portion of the route with an Englishman named Jerym (*Jair-um*) Brunton, whom she knew from the racing circuit. Sixty miles from the finish line, the two enjoyed the first sunny day in a week. They stopped to peel off a few layers of clothing and to enjoy the clear, blue sky. Diane shed her down jacket, a fleece pullover, and a Gore-Tex shirt. Off went her down feather pants, too. She still wore several layers, and she threw the stripped items onto her sled.

And then, the bottom dropped out for Diane.

"I can shut my eyes right now and still remember that sound. The *kkkkkkkkk*. The ice cracking."

The frozen river Diane and Jerym were trekking on gave way.

"I'm out ahead of him, and all of the sudden I hear this *splash*!" Diane says. "I fell through the ice."

Diane was connected to her sled by a hip belt. Because she had lost about eight pounds during the race, the loose belt floated up around her neck instead of yanking the sled along with her into the hole. Diane's trekking poles and arms remained out of the water and she braced herself on the edge of the ice. Thankfully, Jerym was able to pull Diane up and out of the frigid water by reaching out to her with his trekking pole. Her shoes and clothes instantly froze.

"And then I had to think, because I didn't want to get frostbite or become hypothermic. I had just stripped off those other layers, thank

God," Diane explains. "So, I started stripping as fast as I could, and Jerym had an extra T-shirt, so I grabbed that. I didn't carry any other extra clothing because you don't want to pull more weight. The only thing I had was an extra pair of socks. I had baggies on my sled, so I thought, *I'll put a baggie on each of my feet, over the sock, and then I'll put my shoes on so I have a barrier.* That way when my shoes started to melt from the warmth of my body moving, that kept my socks from freezing. That put a huge adrenaline surge into both of us. We just laughed and moved forward."

Diane's level head and quick thinking had propelled her out of a life-threatening situation and back into the game.

"That's the challenge. It's all about the respect. When you're on a ledge with sixty-mile-per-hour winds, and in one fall you're down three miles, there's no, 'We'll come get ya.' It's 'We'll find you in a couple days.' *What am I gonna endure? How am I gonna get through it? Keep your head; don't panic.* And that's really how I got through my seizures."

Diane, Jerym, and every other racer were equipped with tracking devices so family and friends could map their progress along the punishing route. Before competing in the 430, Diane created the Miles for a Mission fund, an exciting way to align the Arctic challenge with fund-raising for patients and families at Craig Hospital, where she received such impactful counseling. Now serving as the hospital's donor relations coordinator, Diane's friend Barb says funds raised are used to help Craig Hospital patients and families affected by spinal cord and traumatic brain injuries.

"Whether it's equipment, whether it's a family member that needs to stay at Craig," Barb explains, "whether it's to help someone build a ramp at their house, whether it's a piece of adaptive sporting equipment, it all helps."

Barb, along with hundreds of coworkers, closely followed Diane's progress in the Yukon each day.

"We could track essentially where she was," says Barb, "and by gosh, we had a fourth of Craig Hospital tracking her and e-mailing each other: 'Where is she? Is she okay?' People just love her."

Only eight competitors went the distance. After eleven days, Diane and Jerym crossed the finish line together, fourth overall. Diane was the first and only woman to complete the harrowing race.

This e-mail from Scott was posted on a Denver sports blog:

An exuberant Diane called home this morning to express her ap-
preciation for all the support and good wishes she received during
this grueling event. The angels on her shoulders had big wings!
Diane walked into Dawson this morning at 4:45 A.M. The GPS
tracking unit started reporting sometime early this morning and
tracked teammate Jerym across the finish line. With satisfaction
and relief, Diane took a long hot shower and will try to get some
sleep. SWEET WIN DIANE! Way to Go Di!!

While the Yukon Arctic Ultra 430 would serve as the race of a lifetime for most athletes, Diane would run four additional ultrama-rathons that year, in Canada, Colorado, Wyoming, and China.

Much has been written about Diane's miraculous ability to run so far and remain so seemingly unfazed by the rigors of ultra com-petition. Some clinicians speculate in articles that removing part of Diane's brain also removed her ability to process pain.

"That's hard for me," Diane says. "The surgery didn't change me or who I am, my stubbornness, my passion. If anything, it's compli-cated my life. The way I prepare for a race is way different than any-body else. They all think, 'Oh, great, you don't feel pain.' Well, shit—I don't feel pain? I feel pain. I just push through it."

Interestingly, Diane had the opportunity in 2009 to see that her tremendous self-determination has always had a running partner: her unique physiology.

At a dinner near Lake Tahoe that year, Diane was chatting with North Face executives gathered for the company's global meetings. She learned that plans were in the works for about ten South American managers to climb Mount Aconcagua in Argentina near the Chilean border. At 22,841 feet, the mountain is the Western Hemisphere's highest point and the second-highest outside of central and southern Asia. Diane had never climbed higher than fifteen thousand feet.

"I was with the South American group and I had a couple of glasses of wine," Diane says with a grin, "and I love my South American group. We're sitting around laughing and embracing life, and Aconcagua came up. And I said, 'I could do a speed attempt up that thing! Let's climb it first and then I'll go for a speed record!'"

Done. Plans began to take shape for a January 2010 expedition in the Andes. Little did everyone know, the guest list was about to expand. At the close of 2009, the December 2009/January 2010 edition of *National Geographic Adventure* named Diane as one of their Adventurers of the Year. Doctors from the Mayo Clinic took note and became interested in her Aconcagua expedition. Mayo had just created the Extreme Medicine and Physiology Program to research why some elite athletes can not only endure but excel under extraordinary stress. The goal was to collect data and apply it to help heart-failure patients. That December, Mayo doctors invited Diane and Scott to their lab in Rochester, Minnesota.

"I said to them, 'If we're gonna do this, why don't you come to Aconcagua, too?'" Diane explains. "So they said, 'Okay, we're gonna test you here in the hospital and then we'll test you on the mountain.' And that's what they were comparing: How am I gonna do in the lab, and then how am I gonna do at twenty-two thousand feet?"

The Mayo team put Diane through three days of baseline tests to compare against the upcoming Aconcagua ascent. Ironically, she had never before run on a treadmill, only outside on trails. Doctors placed electrodes on her body and asked her to run as hard as she could for an hour at a 15 percent grade.

"They had me on a treadmill with twenty pounds on my back and a mask on my face, and they were testing how much oxygen I take in, how far I can go, what my limits are."

For the first time, Diane would get raw data on whether there was something, in addition to her mental toughness, that made her such an athletic badass.

"I knew in my racing I could recover fast, but that was something I learned in the testing," Diane says. "They could push me until I was ready to pass out, but all I had to do was step off the machine, and after they gave me ten seconds, I was ready to go again. So, that's what they found. My recovery rate is just really fast."

Doctors also determined that Diane had a literally breathtaking ability to take in oxygen. Data showed her maximal oxygen intake was about double the average for a woman her age. Diane's lung surface area is about one and a half times the average size.

"Obviously," Diane jokes, "you don't have to have big boobs to have big lungs."

Diane's muscles were determined to be superstars as well, as efficient as those of a woman nearly thirty years younger.

The next step was to leave the lab and gear up for feisty Mount Aconcagua. In January 2010, Diane and nine other climbers were hooked up with electrodes. Real-time medical data would be gathered, stored on laptops, and then wirelessly transmitted back to computers at Mayo. The mission had two parts. The first was to generate data as Diane, the other climbers, and medical staff slowly trekked to the top of the mountain along a treacherous but well-traveled trail. The second goal was to monitor Diane and a fellow elite climber a day or two later as they re-summited as quickly as possible along the same route, or as similar as possible based on weather conditions. Diane's neurologist, Dr. Spitz, offered his blessing when Diane initially inquired about the medical risks of the ultra-high-altitude expedition.

"I'm a big believer in 'live your life,'" Spitz says. "When I look at life, there's a certain amount of risk in everything we do, so I weigh the potential benefits, of course being careful, and is it worth it? I know Diane as a person well. I know how important these things are for her. It's her identity, and so I carefully think about what she's going to be doing, but I tend to let her go for it."

Diane and the team went for it in mid-January. Doctors placed a small harness around the middle of Diane's chest to measure her respiratory and heart rates as well as her oxygen saturation. She was also monitored by a neuropsychologist for cognitive issues related to altitude sickness. The expedition would take weeks, due to the acclimation process and erratic weather conditions. A massive volcanic mountain, Aconcagua is frequently blasted by a hurricane-force jet stream that Argentineans call the *viento blanco,* or white wind.

In a Mayo Clinic blog post from January 30, Diane describes preparing for the summit and for her speed record attempt:

It really was so great to feel awesome climbing to 18,000 feet! Stunning to be on top of the mountain on a crystal clear blue sky day and you could see forever! I told Bruce and Luke [a Mayo doctor and his son] that I think this is a glance of what heaven is going to be like. It was great to climb and feel in my element. No headache, no tightness of lungs etc. Tomorrow we will take gear to camp one and we will not have contact for maybe 6 7 8 days as it depends on weather conditions on the mountain. No summiting today because of the winds. Well, love to everyone and keep prayers for everyone . . . start the summit tomorrow. xo Di

But the first several days of February unleashed sixty-mile-per-hour winds and minus-twenty-degrees temperatures. Climbers could not summit until February 9, and not everyone made it to the top. Diane did, and immediately began to gear up for her next challenge, the speed ascent.

"I promised everyone that the docs would come home alive," Diane explains, "that I wouldn't take any risks."

And that's why Diane made the frustrating but prudent decision to ultimately cancel the speed attempt. Blizzard conditions, high winds, and below-zero temperatures prompted her to call off the mission. The doctors had successfully gathered a wealth of physiological and psychological data on the slow summit; the second mission was too risky.

Interestingly, in Mayo's written insights about the expedition, the lead doctor discusses the elusive challenge of learning why some people have a "well-designed persistence for adaptation." Dr. Bruce Johnson writes, "Why some people keep striving amid life's traumas and others don't is a perplexing issue."

Perplexing indeed. What Diane exhibits as an elite athlete, and has since she was little, will never show up in telemetry data.

"I told the docs I still think it's what's up here." She points to her head. "You can be the fastest athlete in the world, but if you can't use it here," she says, pointing to her head again, "and know how to keep your shit together, you're done. And I really had to keep my shit together when I had my seizures, so I can just keep it together in the moment. It's the push, it's in the head."

Diane lives in Sedalia, Colorado, elk country, forty minutes south of Denver on thirty-five acres, where she and Scott raised their three children. A fifty-two-year-old natural beauty, Diane wears no makeup; she wears her blond hair short and simple. Her skin has been kissed by the sun and battered by winds that blow where few choose to explore. Diane is five feet nine, one hundred and thirty-five pounds—extremely lean but not emaciated. In a constant state of motion since she was young, Diane's never comfortable at rest.

But in December 2011, she had no choice. Diane was ordered to sit in a chair with her right leg prone and to heal. She had endured a severely painful procedure on a torn Achilles tendon. Doctors and therapists who work with Denver's professional sports teams were tasked with getting Diane's tendon to properly heal using an experimental technique, the kind of procedure that makes even the toughest athletes cry or use expletives. By the third session, with several more to go, Diane was in bad shape and using bad language.

"I was crawling around the house. I was holding my leg," she describes, "lying on the floor, cussing my head off."

In an office setting, doctors drew blood from Diane, separated out the pristine red blood cells, drew them into a syringe, and, without numbing her, injected the needle into her Achilles on both sides of her heel. The technique is designed to promote circulation and healing. The injury was debilitating to Diane's race schedule and her psyche. By now you know that she's not an elite relaxer. To make matters worse, the ankle injury was not caused by running.

In 2009, Diane had headed out for a routine predawn trail run. "It was four o'clock in the morning and I was headed for a trail no one even knows about," Diane says, "and I get out of my car in the parking lot, and all of a sudden this guy flips on his headlamp and says, 'Get the fuck outta here.' I turned off my headlamp, and as I was running out of there, I jumped a fence and my foot went into an old fence post hole, and when I pulled out my foot, that's when I strained it."

Diane hid herself and called the police.

"I could see him loading the gun"—she makes the clicking sound of cocking a gun—"looking around for me, looking in my car. I was lying in the grass thinking, *Get here, get here, get here.*"

Police, who arrived forty-five minutes later, think Diane walked up on a drug deal. They were never able to track down the gunman. Diane raced every month after the injury, so it never got a chance to heal.

"I told my friend that if I ever see that son of a bitch again," she says jokingly, "I ain't running from him next time . . . I'm taking him down!"

Extreme physical therapy instead of extreme physical exercise was an exasperating tradeoff for Diane. She was limited to pool workouts and core exercises. And lots of quality time with fear.

"There was an underlying, *Wow, what am I gonna do now?* This sport has been so good to me."

So good, and so time consuming. The sport requires an immense time commitment. Diane's typical day unfolds early. While the coffee brews, she laces up one of the fifteen pairs of running shoes she wears out each year. Out the door by around four A.M., Diane grabs a quick carbohydrate (like a muffin) and eats it in her lap while driving. She often heads to Pikes Peak, altitude 14,110 feet. Up she runs, fourteen miles to the summit.

"I'll throw a headlamp on, run up to the top, and I'll stay up there for a while for altitude training," she says. "I'll run a bunch of back trails that no one knows about, so I have the whole mountain to myself. It's kinda nice."

Hours later, when Diane decides to head back down the mountain, she'll text her friend who works with search and rescue in Colorado Springs. The potential for a bear encounter or a fall is real, so she wants someone to know where she's training. After logging twenty to thirty miles by noon, Diane heads home for lunch, always carbs and protein to refuel the repair of tissue breakdown from her intense workout. Her calorie burn for the day easily reaches six to seven thousand, so her lunch will include an entire bag of mixed vegetables that she microwaves, along with tofu, tuna, or chicken and Greek yogurt. After lunch, Diane tackles e-mails and details on clothing design for the North Face. She may also need to prepare a presentation for her work as a North Face traveling speaker. Dinner for her and Scott probably cooked all day in a Crock-Pot (less chance of burning) or is a simple preparation of fish, salad, and baked potatoes or rice.

"After dinner I go for the cereal and the ice cream. That's where the sweet craving comes in. I don't even put it in a bowl. I just grab the whole carton and . . ." She makes slurping sounds.

Diane is usually in bed by eight thirty P.M., the structured life of a professional athlete. It is not lost on Diane how fortunate she's been to have a loving, strong, patient, capable life partner in Scott. At six feet four, he's never lived his life in Diane's shadow literally or figuratively. He's steadfastly and graciously handled the role of husband, father, mother, and cheerleader.

"He's always been my knight in shining armor," Diane says. "How many men would handle a wife seizing, three small children, and having to play the role of mom when I was late picking up the kids? And try to live a normal life?"

Their married life, like most, has not been without challenges. Diane says even after nearly thirty years together, they're still ironing out the dynamics of their relationship, plus the one they share with a brain injury.

"We've struggled in our marriage with my injury, just like with any other marriage. And he's been shortchanged—let's be honest— because I'd be out running all the time," she shares, "and he honored that, and he let me be that, but I need to make sure I make time for him."

Several years ago they went through couples' therapy with a close friend who works in the field. She helped them both better understand how a traumatic brain injury can promote anger when there is confusion. Diane says she always thought she was handling family and married life well but realized through therapy what those around her have had to manage.

"There were times when I was so frustrated and confused. 'Scott, why didn't you tell me about that?' Or 'Why are you doing all this stuff, taking over for the kids? I can do that!' He would tell me something and I'd forget it. It became very stressful." Then she jokes, "I always said the best marriage would be two brain injury patients because no one can remember shit. If you got into a fight, the next day, you'd both be like, 'Did I say that? Really? What did you say?' Scott and I could have a disagreement and the next day he'd be stewing and I'd just be oblivious, like, 'What's the problem?'"

Diane calls their marriage a loving work in progress. She's determined to make more time for Scott and to ask for his help in areas where she now realizes she needs it. Scott says they're still learning how to get what they need from each other after twenty-nine years of marriage.

"There is no bigger fan than me because I understand the hard work she puts in. It's incredible. So, there is no bigger fan, but sometimes I don't want to be her fan, I want to be her husband."

Diane acknowledges that she unintentionally caused hurt in their marriage.

"What he's been through as a husband has been very difficult. I couldn't ask for a better man. He's the best husband, the best father; there's nobody who could fill his shoes. I am so blessed. He's really had to step up to the plate." She pauses. "Talk about endurance."

How *has* Scott managed to support Diane so often and for so long? The question makes him emotional.

"I have this vision in my head of what a family and what an incredible marriage could be," he says, choking up, "and I just want to do my part. I go back to that Amelia Earhart example, and I don't want to be the guy on the History Channel that they talk about, 'Well, yeah, Amelia Earhart was supposed to do all these great things and fly, but her husband didn't want her to.' So, there's something special about Diane and she's in my life for a reason, and we're pretty incredible together. I don't have all the answers, but somewhere in there is my vision."

Mike, Diane, Scott, Robin, Matt. Sedalia, Colorado, 2010.
(Courtesy of Diane Van Deren)

In an effort to spare others from experiencing the painful lessons she's learned about life with a brain injury, Diane has often counseled other people living with the same challenge. In early 2010, Diane met thirty-eight-year-old Jake Quigley, a candidate for the same brain surgery that ended her seizures. Jake was referred to Diane by a colleague he works with at a nonprofit organization. Over the course of more than six months, she guided him through the difficult decision of whether to undergo the surgery. They talked through the uncertainty, what to expect from the surgery, what to anticipate throughout the recovery process, and how the successful outcome impacted her quality of life. Diane also shared with Jake that his twenty-seven years of seizures had not only damaged his brain but could also be damaging to his relationship with his wife.

"I told him how he needs to hold his wife's hand sometimes," Diane says, "and look her in the eyes and thank her."

Jake decided to undergo the surgery, and in April 2011, four months after his successful operation, he sent Diane a handwritten letter. Along with the note, he sent her a cowbell. The letter explained why:

> *When I was a kid, my winter months were spent playing hockey at the rink across from my house in Watertown, Connecticut. My father and mother would always come to my games to watch me play. My mother would bring this cowbell to each of my games and ring it fiercely each time I took the ice.*

The letter goes on to explain that when Jake was a senior in high school, he sustained a devastating blow. His mother died in a raging fire that burned down the family house. At his high school graduation, Jake's family presented him with a special gift: the cowbell. They'd found it in the burned rubble and had it cleaned and polished for him. Jake treasured it throughout his life. He shared these words with Diane:

> *I have been fortunate to meet you this past year. In many ways you have influenced me with your optimism, strength, and determination. You have been generous to guide me through the journey of opting to have surgery and facing the fears and potential complications. Your experience, honesty, and support allowed me to maintain a positive outlook throughout the process. Please accept this gift as a symbol of my gratitude for your friendship and positive influence. I wanted to give you*

something meaningful. The cowbell can also be a motivator at
future races!

Your friend, Jake

For all of Diane's amazing accomplishments in the sports world,
it's her impact off the running trails that matters most to her. Training
and competing is second nature, but Diane is determined to work as
diligently at maintaining connections with family, friends, and fellow
victims of disabilities. Along with her Miles for a Mission fund, Diane
has also helped raise money for the epilepsy camp for children that
inspired her to keep running long distances. As a North Face athlete,
she speaks to groups across the country, as well as abroad, eight to ten
times a year. Audience members often share with Diane their personal
experience with seizures, or their children's struggles with epilepsy, or
fears about an approaching surgery similar to the one Diane underwent. She's grateful to listen and offer what they may be seeking.

"I think a little bit of hope," says Diane. "Wanting to see a positive side, knowing we all have obstacles, we're not perfect. They want
to think, *Maybe I can try, too,* or *Gosh, maybe what I have isn't that bad,*
or *Thanks for motivating me.*"

Diane is grateful for the chance to share what she's learned. She's
also relieved to have sorted through the past with her family. She now
knows that her brain wasn't the only thing scarred by her seizures.

"For my mom's seventy-fifth birthday, we took her downtown
and we stayed in a nice hotel," Diane says. "She made the comment
that she still has a hard time looking at me, because for so many years
she used to watch me to make sure my eyes didn't glaze or show signs
of trouble."

I ask Diane about her own imprinted fear. Does she still worry
about having a seizure?

"I think about it sometimes, sure. When I'm in the Yukon, in the middle of nowhere, it's fifty below, there's a little reminder there. When I'm hallucinating and pushing, there's a little mouse behind me saying, 'Be smart.'"

Diane's 2011 Achilles injury got her thinking about the day that her body won't allow her to run ultramarathons anymore.

"I told Scott, my only problem is I get bored. I love being in the middle of everything. I love action, so I need to find that next step. I need to embrace what I can still do and what I've done," she says. "I've done the longest and the coldest and the hardest. What more is there?"

Oh, there's more. Don't let her fool you.

In October 2011, Diane was speaking in Raleigh, North Carolina, representing the North Face. Tickets to the event benefited a local nonprofit organization trying to raise money to further develop a foot trail across the entire state. The Mountains-to-Sea Trail stretches nearly one thousand miles, from Clingman's Dome in the Great Smoky Mountains to Jockey's Ridge on the Outer Banks. The diverse route ranges from the third-tallest mountain peak in the eastern United States to the largest natural sand dune on the East Coast. The trail passes through thirty-seven counties and three national parks, and meanders by three lighthouses, including the nation's tallest, the Cape Hatteras Lighthouse. Three ferry rides are required.

The group's efforts to generate exposure for the trail piqued Diane's curiosity.

"And I said, 'Well, anybody ever run it?'"

Uh-huh. You know where this is going. Organizers told her that only one man had speed-trekked the trail, and he did it in twenty-four days. That was all Diane needed to hear. She proposed the expedition to the North Face, it was approved, and her goal was to complete it in twenty-one days. She'd need to run an average of more than forty miles per day with several days of fifty-plus-mile runs.

On June 1, 2012, at fifty-two years old, Diane completed the Mountains-to-Sea Trail expedition in twenty-two days, five hours, and three minutes, breaking the old record of twenty-four days, three hours, and fifty minutes set in 2011 by North Carolinian Matt Kirk, twenty-two years younger than Diane. Following a May 10 start from Clingman's Dome in the Appalachians, Diane trekked nearly one thousand miles across North Carolina, reaching the Atlantic Ocean and Jockey's Ridge State Park on June 1 at 9:29 A.M. EDT. She calls it the hardest expedition she's ever completed.

"The pain was excruciating," Diane says. "I'm really good at focusing on the task and not being distracted, but I've never had to dig so deep and deal with so many emotions and try to stay levelheaded for so long."

For Diane, the golden moment came not at the finish, but two miles out. She gathered the eight people—all volunteers—who'd been with her the entire journey, who'd made her victory possible. She asked them to form a circle.

"I just wanted to gather everybody and hold hands, and I just went into prayer to thank God for the journey, and the gifts, and the gift of life, the beauty he had shown through every person who was with me," she recalls. "We were all together and holding hands and crying; you could just hear tears hitting the concrete. There was this photographer who had been following me all the way—in-my-face kind of stuff—and I thought, *You know what? If we're gonna give him a shot, let's give him this*. That circle of love, that circle of life, that circle of overcoming everything we came through, was right there. That was really powerful. That one picture, that one shot of us all holding hands, is probably the best memory I'll have."

Scott flew to Raleigh to meet Diane a few hours after she finished.

"When he took me to the hotel room, it just felt so good to put my arms around him, to be in bed and feel his body next to mine. My legs were just hurting so bad, and he rubbed my legs all night. He knew what to do. That was just so comforting to me. To be in bed with my husband. That was the moment when I was like, *Wow, I'm done.*"

Diane describes the thousand-miler as being her one last Big Daddy accomplishment. But don't look for a rocking chair on her front porch just yet.

"I don't think so." She adds jokingly, "If I'm in one it's because I'm on medication."

For now, as always, she's focused on whatever is around the next rugged bend.

"I'm so much an in-the-moment person. I can think forward a day or two, maybe a week, but if you get so set on your goals, you miss the other opportunities," she says. "And that's what I've always told the kids: 'You can have your goals but don't miss the right turn, left turn, right turn,' because that's where our character and confidence and self-esteem come from."

If you ask Diane what else she hopes her kids have learned from her and what she'd like her legacy to be, her answer is straightforward.

"Live your dream. Believe in yourself. You can do it. You just gotta try. Embrace life."

The words line up like even steps along a mountain trail. They are positive and powerful, just like Diane.

RON CLIFFORD

In September 2001, I was assigned a *Dateline NBC* story for a network special highlighting the horrific aftermath of 9/11. My job was to interview Ron Clifford, just a few days after he suffered tremendous loss in the wake of the terrorist attacks. When he walked into the small room we had set up as a studio, we exchanged hellos and Ron asked me about the origin of my name. My heart dropped, knowing his had just been broken by people from the Middle East. When I replied, "Egypt," Ron told me to stand up. I slowly stood, wondering if, in his searing pain, he was about to lash out at me. Instead, Ron threw his arms around me. He hugged me close and told me that he loved Anwar Sadat and the Egyptian culture. That was just the start of my immense respect and love for Ron Clifford. It grows each time I sit down to talk with him.

◆◇◆◉◆◇◆

Ron Clifford grew up in southeastern Ireland in the lush city of Cork. The centuries-old Irish seaport is blessed with rivers, bays, and one of the world's largest natural harbors. With easy access to both fresh and salt water, the Clifford family always owned speedboats and cabin cruisers. One of five children, Ron was raised with his older brother,

John, his younger sister, Ruth, and two younger brothers, Gordon and Mark. Their home was constantly bustling with neighborhood friends of all ages. Mr. Clifford, a paper merchant, often took his kids camping, waterskiing, and fishing. He taught them all to crew and sail on neighbors' sailboats. Ron clearly loved his brothers, but just a year apart in age from Ruth, he developed a particularly close relationship with his sister. They shared mutual friends and enjoyed spending time together.

"She wasn't allowed out of the house at night without me," Ron says. "We were both fun seekers."

During their early teens, Ruth and Ron loved to sneak out for a joyride in their dad's car. They'd cruise the back roads of Cork at night.

"And then at two or three o'clock in the morning, we'd push it back in the driveway. We were in it together, and we would sometimes pick up friends and take off somewhere in the car."

Ron and Ruth had an easy relationship. They loved to laugh and talk, and she was known in the neighborhood as a compassionate girl, the one who would drop off food to a family when someone was sick.

"I was always just proud that I had a sister like her," Ron says. "It was always fun to be with her."

When the kids were teens and preteens, their parents separated and, after several years, divorced. Dad stayed with the children; Mom moved to Dublin to take care of her ailing mother. For a year, the sole female influence in the family was Ruth. She often mothered her brothers, and they listened.

"It wasn't us arriving on our motorcycles to a dance." Ron shakes his pointer finger as if it's his sister's. "Ruth made sure we wore ties and behaved ourselves." He smiles. "We were kind of crude with our jokes, but you'd never do that in front of Ruth."

In the family kitchen, Ruth was an accomplished and creative cook.

"She could take one peek in the fridge and figure out how to make a gourmet meal."

During high school, the brothers were willing guinea pigs for Ruth's culinary pursuits. Ron remembers his sister perfecting a dish she entered in a competition (which she won) hosted by Ireland's fisheries board.

"Haddock à la crème. It was spectacular!" he recalls. "We would beg her to experiment with us. She displayed it on silver platters with mandarin oranges. It was a judge's delight."

In 1973, in order to be with her new husband, Ron's mom moved to the United States, taking seventeen-year-old Ruth with her. Just a year later, the already fractured family would experience acute misery. The second-youngest brother, Gordon, was killed on his way home from secondary school in Ireland.

"Gordon was sixteen and had just bought a new motorbike after working all summer," Ron explains. "He ended up being pushed off the road by an elderly driver." The impact was lethal. "He hit his head severely and ultimately died."

Just twenty, Ron did his best to support his father through the anguishing decision to terminate life support for Gordon. They chose to donate his organs, a decision, they later learned, that saved two people's lives.

For five years, Ruth and her mother lived in the U.S. and Ron and his brothers remained in Cork. But growing political unrest and the declining Irish economy forced Ron to also consider a move to the States. He decided to visit Ruth in Rochester, New York, where she lived along with their mom. After the two-month visit and with encouragement from Ruth, Ron decided to make a life in America. In 1978, at twenty-four, Ron returned to the U.S. on a visa and worked on a farm west of Rochester managing cattle and restoring barns. Nine months later, he returned to Ireland to get his relocation papers in order. In May 1980, Ron immigrated to America, returning to the farm to work and live in a home the landowner offered him. Three years later, Ron's passion for structural design led him to enroll in college at the Boston Architectural Center. Before graduating, he took a job heading up the computer-aided design group for the New York City Housing Authority.

Ruth spent those same years attending college in Rochester, followed by a position with a modeling school opening new branches around the country. She then moved overseas to London to apprentice with a renowned skin care specialist, learning the art of postoperative cosmetics. By 1986, Ruth had returned to the States and, in a suburb of Boston, opened a day spa. She would eventually launch her own line of skin care products. Several years into her spa and salon business, Ruth struck up a friendship with a client named Paige Hackel. The two immediately became best friends, sharing a love for gardening, entertaining, and worldwide travel.

In 1988, Ron married his wife, Brigid, whom he'd dated for two years. They first met when Brigid picked up the phone at a Boston apartment where a party was under way, hosted by mutual friends.

"I called for directions and she answered the phone," he says with a laugh, "and we've been on speaking terms ever since."

Two years into their marriage, in 1990, Ron and Brigid started a family in New Jersey. Brigid gave birth to a daughter, Monica. Within the first hours of her life, Monica was battling for it. She'd been born with throat complications that required immediate surgery and recovery in the neonatal unit.

"I was just praying that my child wasn't one of the children that was going to die that night," says Ron.

The newborn spent three months in intensive care. When Monica finally came home, Brigid began the arduous process of teaching her baby how to eat and swallow. Feedings could take two hours. For years, the risk of her aspirating food and liquids was high.

"The care Brigid gave Monica was unbelievable," Ron says, marveling. "We were always back and forth to the hospital, and we slept on her bedroom floor with her for two or three years."

Ron says both sides of the family were remarkable in their support. Ruth frequently flew in from Boston to help and sent countless care packages for Monica as she grew up and grew stronger. After several years, Monica's health improved and she no longer was in danger.

In September of 1994, it was Ruth's turn to marry. She wed David McCourt, who was introduced to her by mutual friends. She sold her business and moved to New London, Connecticut, David's hometown. Three years later, Ruth gave birth to a daughter, Juliana. Ruth selected her best friend, Paige, as Juliana's godmother. For Juliana, she chose the middle name "Valentine," the first name of Ron and Ruth's father, who died suddenly several days before Ruth's wedding. The two had shared a special bond.

"Dad called Ruth his Strawberry Blonde." Ron chuckles. "My brothers told me in the weeks before Ruth would go back to Ireland for vacation, Dad would put this Grecian Formula in his hair"—Ron pretends to use a comb—"to look good for Ruth!"

Ruth, Ron, and the two other brothers spent their busy adult lives growing businesses and raising children. With both their father and brother deceased, everyone did their best to stay connected and to gather for vacations and holidays. Ron describes Ruth as "the glue"; she sent plane tickets to family when needed and remembered every birthday. Each autumn, Ruth would send a packet of fall leaves to John, Ron, and Mark, with a note saying it was time to reflect on their lives.

"There's an old Irish adage that says, 'The Irish guy *nearly* told his wife he loved her.'" Ron laughs and repeats it with a "*neeeearly*." "Ruth showed us what love was and how to express love. We talked about love and the poetry of life. She had a very deep sense of love and caring."

In the fall of 2001, Ron heard from Ruth that she'd planned yet another fun getaway with Paige and his now four-year-old niece.

Their plan was to fly to California to see friends and to surprise Juliana with a visit to Disneyland.

Juliana and Ruth. August 2001. (Courtesy of Ron Clifford)

Days earlier, Ron had spoken with Ruth by phone about an important work meeting he had scheduled in New York City for Tuesday, September 11. He was at home in New Jersey; she was at home in Connecticut, getting ready for her mini vacation on the West Coast. Always the loving cheerleader, Ruth advised Ron to dress for success.

"Ruth told me to wear a bright tie. She told me to wear a bright yellow tie to this meeting," Ron recalls.

As always, Ron heeded his sister's advice. He bought a yellow tie and a new suit. A software executive, Ron's goal for the breakfast meeting was to bring together two rival companies.

"I got a call around six o'clock in the morning," Ron says, "saying the meeting was moved from the midtown Marriott to the Marriott World Trade Center. That excited me because it gave me a chance to take the ferry over from home, take a deep breath, and enjoy the lovely morning."

It was an important day both professionally and personally. Ron wanted the meeting to go well, and quickly, so he could get back home to celebrate his daughter's "golden birthday." Monica was turning eleven on the eleventh of September.

At eight thirty A.M., Ron arrived at the Marriott hotel, nestled between the Twin Towers. With half an hour to spare, he walked from the hotel into the lobby of the World Trade Center. Having studied architecture in college and worked for the housing authority, Ron was always interested in absorbing the dramatic details of a structure.

"I was just walking around the lobby," says Ron. "I was always amazed by how high the arches were and the spans these windows had gained with such a high building."

Fifteen minutes later, as Ron casually walked back into the hotel lobby, his world was literally rocked.

"There was a boom. And I could smell what I thought was paraffin, kerosene," Ron describes, both palms waving toward his nose. "I didn't put it together that it was aviation fuel. I just thought it must have been a ruptured pipe in the basement or something. The building shook, and there was a haze, and people were running. There was chaos."

Ron says no one could gauge what had happened. The lobby was thick with smoke, ash, and confusion.

"All of the sudden, out of the haze, I saw this woman who was extremely badly burned"—Ron squints—"but I couldn't figure out why she was burned or how she was burned. She couldn't see, and I just said, 'C'mon, let me help you.'"

The injured woman was thirty-eight-year-old Jennieann Maffeo, a computer analyst with Paine Webber. She'd stumbled in from the street through the revolving doors of the hotel after being showered with burning aviation fuel as she waited for a bus.

"I remember she had a barrette in her hair and it was melted in," Ron says, touching the top of his head, "and she had a zipper on her sweater and it was melted, too. And the tops of her shoes were burned off."

Ron grabbed a trash can with a fresh plastic liner and filled it with water in a nearby restroom. He gently doused Jennieann's burns. Ron's calls for help were drowned out by the initial wave of tumult. After several minutes, a woman in a red blazer approached them (Ron would learn later she was a nurse from the Marriott), offering gauze pads and oxygen. In the frenzy of people running by, Ron managed to stop a man with a coat, asking him to please hold it in front of the severely burned and naked woman whose clothes had been burned off.

Ron tried to pass time until further help arrived. He asked Jennieann her name and her boss's name. He wrote down the information and also her medical allergies on a notepad he had in a pocket.

"She said to me, 'Please don't tell my parents, they're elderly,'" Ron recalls. "'Please, Sacred Heart of Jesus, please don't let me die.'"

Ron asked Jennieann if she was Catholic, and when she nodded, he suggested they pray together. He told her he thought she was going to be okay.

"So, we were saying the Lord's Prayer and—I'll remember this until the day I die—there was another explosion. And the floor jumped up and the building just shook incredibly. It was as if someone just grabbed you and shook you," Ron says, both fists clenched, shaking the air.

Ron quickly helped Jennieann to her feet and told her they had to get out of the building.

"I remember the panic in me then, thinking, *This is not right.*" He did not like what he was seeing or hearing from the stressed building. "Pieces of ceiling were falling down, pieces of glass; there seemed to be a wind blowing through the building."

Another man offered to help Ron, and together, with Jennieann's hands covered in gauze and oxygen flowing, they began walking through the lobby toward the street.

"We got up to the center of the lobby, and there was a big burly waiter, and I said to him, 'Can you give me a big, big tablecloth?' So he threw me a large, white tablecloth and I wrapped it around her."

Ron and several helpers had managed to get Jennieann, burned over 90 percent of her body, out onto the street. The view from outside of the building took Ron's breath away.

"It was gray. There was a big UPS or FedEx truck that had been incinerated, and I looked up," Ron continues quietly, "and the building was just dripping. Pieces of iron were falling down and there were ashes everywhere." He takes a deep breath, almost smelling the day again.

Someone alerted the small group assisting Jennieann to an ambulance across the West Side Highway. They began to move forward, despite the sensory assault of deafening noise and terrible smells.

"This fireman was coming toward us," says Ron. "He had on a white hat, a big guy. And he said, 'For Jesus Christ's sake, run! Fucking run!'"

They moved as quickly as possible. During the frantic quest toward help, Ron repeatedly heard a sound he couldn't place.

"Every so often you'd hear," Ron says with both hands elevated, "*sheeee-woosh.*" His hands drop down in unison. He adds softly, "I had no idea what it was. All I wanted to do was to get this woman to an ambulance."

Ron with Jennieann. September 11, 2001.
(Credit: New York Daily News/GETTY Images)

When they finally spotted help, Ron gave the information he'd gathered about Jennieann to the emergency medical workers.

A video exists that Ron opted not to view, but his family did. They watched it and told him of the amazing confirmation of his story. Irish television had interviewed Ron for a 9/11 documentary and had obtained a color photo of Ron helping Jennieann, wrapped in a tablecloth, onto the street. Miraculously, producers also obtained FBI surveillance video from a downtown building camera that captures Ron, alongside Jennieann, as her gurney is loaded into an ambulance. That yellow tie. It's captured on tape. Ron's special yellow tie, worn for a morning full of promise that turned into the worst day of his life.

After they loaded Jennieann safely into the ambulance, Ron began walking down the street. For the first time, he took a good look at the buildings. It was then that he realized the ghastly nature of the odd noise. People were jumping from the blazing buildings. Like frames of a horror movie, the bizarre images were seared into his memory.

"I couldn't believe it," Ron says, looking off into space. "I still have these visions of a woman who jumped with her purse. I could see her holding on to her purse. I could see couples jumping hand in hand."

Dazed, Ron made his way through the trappings of catastrophe and asked strangers for any news of what had happened. They told him that two commercial jetliners had hit the towers. Ron was now one of millions of people making the mental transition from acci- dent to terrorist attack. He tried to call Brigid, but cell service was unavailable. Hoping his calling card would work, Ron ran into the American Express building. He'd often taken friends and family on tours of the city and always brought them into the Amex building to see the paintings displayed in the lobby. He knew there was a row of phone banks right inside the doors. Ron was joined in the building by milling emergency workers. A gentleman wearing a police badge stood at the phones and told Ron he didn't have any change to make a call. Ron dialed his AT&T 800 number for the man, then used it on a neighboring phone to call Brigid.

"I said, 'Brigid, I'm down here, I'm okay, I'm looking at it, I will be home. I know the trains are going to run. I'm going to try to get home for Monica's birthday.'"

Brigid told Ron how relieved she was that he was okay. They spoke for just a few minutes, Ron managing a mix of relief and dis- belief as he watched people dive off the towers to their deaths.

When he hung up the phone, Ron reached down to pick up his briefcase. His intent was to leave, but his body slumped to the ground. For a moment, he sat frozen, watching the jumpers and watching people pray and scream as they witnessed the same ap- palling images.

Ron had no way of knowing the worst was yet to come.

Having worked for the city housing authority, Ron knew there was a contingency plan in place by the Port Authority of New York and New Jersey in the event of a disaster. Ferries would leave from the New York side and transport people to Hoboken on the New Jersey side, where they would board trains. The trains would stop at every station on every rail line that New Jersey Transit serviced. Ron told Brigid his plan was to make his way to Hoboken and take a train toward home. He first had to run one block square to get to the ferry that would cross the Hudson. He nearly missed the boat.

"I literally jumped over the gate and got on the ferry. Everybody was stunned. One Asian chap had a piece of the airplane and was showing it off." Ron says, "Everyone wanted to kill him. They were like, 'You are disgusting.'"

Ron was riding on the upper deck of the jam-packed ferry. Panicked people were crying, praying, and trying desperately to make cell phone calls. As the vessel was reaching the other side of the river, he looked back at Manhattan.

"And the first building went down," remembers Ron. "My heart sank. I was horrified. I tried to call Brigid and I couldn't, so she thought I was still down there. In the middle of it."

Off the ferry and now aboard a train toward home, Ron was surrounded by people using BlackBerries to gather and share the latest developments. Ron watched a woman drink several shots of vodka as news spread that the Pentagon had been hit and another plane had crashed in a field. He still had no luck contacting his wife. The normally twenty-minute ride, with added stops, took two hours. Five minutes before his stop, Ron reached Brigid. She raced to meet him at the station.

"She was just in pieces. I was delighted to see her," says Ron. "I had burned skin all over my coat and I smelled like aviation fuel. I was in shock."

When they got home, Monica was still at school. Brigid had not wanted to pick her up before she knew Ron's fate. She told him that his brother-in-law, David, had called saying he couldn't find Ruth.

"Oh, she's in California. She's fine," Ron told her, assuming his sister, Paige, and Juliana had left that weekend for their Disney trip. He would call David after taking a much-needed shower. But David's call alarmed Ron. Instead of showering, he decided to call Paige's husband, Alan. He had shocking news.

"Alan said to me, 'Ron, Paige's plane hit the World Trade Center, but Ruth wasn't on the plane.'" Ron sighs and says, "I thought, *Thank God*."

But an unimaginable story was about to unfold by the hour. Reality would sink in slowly and, like quicksand, immobilize the families and ultimately suffocate them with grief.

All morning, Ron's two brothers in Ireland had been calling Brigid to see if Ron was okay. He called them back and told them he was fine but that Ruth was missing. Savvy with computers, Ron began to track his sister's whereabouts. He scoured the Internet, searching for flight schedules and airline records. Alan told him that Ruth and Juliana had stayed at Paige's house the night prior to their trip; therefore, they'd flown out of Boston, not Connecticut. He called his stepbrother, who lived in Boston, and told him to set up camp at Logan International Airport and gather any news he could. Ron tracked down the young girl who worked part-time for his sister as a personal assistant. She gave him Ruth's flight numbers. Hours later, the official passenger lists were released, and Ron's worst fears stared back at him from the computer screen.

"I was in my office upstairs on the second floor," says Ron, who has since moved his office up one floor to escape the memories. "I remember pacing around the room," he says as he looks up to the ceiling, "just in agony within the four walls, going, 'No, no, tell me it isn't true.'"

But it was. Ron dreaded his next move: the heartbreaking call to John and Mark, three thousand miles away.

"It's not looking good," Ron said to his brothers. "We're in trouble, I think." He pauses. "It was very hard to tell them. They were devastated."

Shortly after eight A.M., American Airlines Flight 11 departed from Logan International and headed nonstop to Los Angeles. Ruth's best friend, Paige, forty-six, was aboard the flight. The first boom Ron heard in the lobby that morning was Paige's plane slamming into the North Tower.

Ten minutes after the American flight took off, United Flight 175, also nonstop to Los Angeles, departed. Ruth, forty-five, and Juliana, four, were aboard. The friends had flown separately to take advantage of their different frequent-flyer programs. Ron had no idea, as he was jolted by the second explosion, that a plane had hit the second tower, and it was carrying his sister and niece.

"You couldn't even put that into a novel," says Ron, still amazed. "People would be like, 'That's bullshit.'" He raises both eyebrows. "And then to have Monica's birthday, to be eleven on 9/11. You know, September 11. That's the other oddity."

Odd. Horrific. Devastating. Is it possible for a person to endure such a crushing onslaught of loss, grief, and anger? The world changed at the very same moment Ron's world collapsed.

TEN YEARS LATER

It's a crisp October day in 2011. When I walk toward the steps leading up to his stately white house in a suburb of New Jersey, Ron greets me like an old friend. We haven't seen each other in a decade.

"You made it!" he calls out, heading for me with a smile.

We meet on the cement steps. Ron pecks me on the cheek, hugs me, and jokes with a hint of an Irish lilt that he's grown a bit more haggard and robust. We laugh, and as he opens the front screen door for me, a mini Lassie bounds out barking, friendly and curious.

"You okay with dogs?" he asks.

She's Penny, Ron's sheltie. The breed, like all of his beloved treasures, has roots in a land engulfed by the cold waters of the North Atlantic. Ron's strawberry blond hair and white sideburns form a ring around his head; a few holdouts on top connect both sides. His eyes are bright blue, even behind a pair of rimless glasses. The fifty-seven-year-old is wearing navy blue dress pants and a blue pin-striped button-down. He's been working on this Friday, October 14, in his third-floor office.

"The kitchen isn't done yet," Ron says with a big grin, leading me into his 124-year-old home, a work in progress.

Ron and Brigid have renovated several houses throughout their twenty-four-year marriage. But I've come to ask Ron about his journey to reconstruct his life. About the day it all came crashing down. About where the hell someone finds blueprints to lay a new foundation and rebuild the walls of a completely demolished heart and mind. Ten years later, I once again sit down across from Ron.

We're set up in the Cliffords' cozy living room. Brigid is not home but has left a tray of cheerful pastries for us. Ron has brewed coffee and tea. Monica, newly twenty-one, is home, too, visiting with a girl-friend upstairs. Since Ron flew to Ireland for the tenth anniversary of the attacks, he agreed to meet me after his return in October. I ask him to share details about the days and weeks following our 2001 *Dateline* interview.

"Ruth had a friend in public relations who knew Connie Chung," Ron begins, "so this PR machine sort of jumped in there, and before I knew it I was on *Larry King Live*. It was just crazy and mad."

With no recovered remains, the families organized funerals for Ruth, Juliana, and Paige within several days after 9/11.

Drawing in a deep breath, Ron says, "We weren't getting the time to grieve. And I wasn't sleeping. I knew if I shut my eyes I would see these people jumping, and I would see Jennieann. I couldn't deal with it."

In the weeks after the attack, support was pouring in for the families in the form of hams and phone calls. A woman Ron had helped years earlier to garner support from the Shriners for her sick granddaughter called to ask if there was anything she could do and said that her son was a New York City police officer. She wanted to return Ron's favor. When the young officer called, Ron asked him if going down to the World Trade Center site was a possibility.

"He said, 'Look, I can't take you down there, but I'll go down and tell you what it's like.'" Ron adds, "When he came back, he had a piece of glass, and he had a branch of a tree, and he said, 'This is to show you that there is life down there, Ron.'"

Still clinging to life was Jennieann Maffeo, unconscious and battling critical burns over most of her body. Knowing the Maffeos were suffering through the same hell as he and his family were, Ron visited the burn unit several times. On the first visit, he left behind on Jennieann's bed his ravaged yellow tie, a reminder of their connection as survivors.

"Her dad was this lovely little Italian man—from Italy—and he just threw his arms around me and said, 'Thank you for giving me my daughter back,'" Ron says. "He said, 'A lot of people didn't get their children back.'"

Even if it was only for forty days. As Ron was driving home one afternoon, he heard on the radio that Jennieann had died.

"I was devastated. I pulled over to the side of the road. I sat in my car and cried." He tips his head back, looks upward, and says, "God. That was the hope, y'know?"

Mustering what little strength he had left, he attended Jennieann's wake. Ron says he experienced a full-blown panic attack and had to leave early. Agony weighed like an invisible anvil on his heart and mind.

"I was getting very aggravated with lack of sleep and the world was caving in. I was crying like a baby every day; something would set me off," Ron explains. "If anyone started up a motorbike or anything, I would shiver. I couldn't take the loud noise. If I put my head on the pillow, I could see these people jumping and falling. I couldn't watch the twenty-four/seven television coverage. Everything was a reminder. I wanted to get out of where I was at that point. I just didn't know how to deal with it all."

Brigid's sister-in-law put Ron in touch with a New Jersey therapist who specialized in treating clients with battle fatigue. Ron had clearly experienced battlefield conditions and was exhibiting the signs of post-traumatic stress disorder. Ron refers to the therapist as Dr. Doug and smiles when he relays that the doctor, Doug Martinez, claims he's half-Irish. Dr. Doug and Ron met three times a week for six months, exploring Ron's frightening daily existence. "I would look at a newspaper and just see dripping blood," Ron says.

The ultimate goal was to have Ron talk through every moment of that ugly morning. Thirty seconds of terror could take the pair three days to discuss. Ron forced his mind to retrace every step.

"Walking through all that grayness reminded me I was walking through skulls and bodies. It was like in the movie *Schindler's List*, and I was scrubbing my feet every night in the shower until they bled. I knew this was just not me. I was in a really bad place."

Even sailing, which Ron had enjoyed since childhood, was

threatened by his toxic mental state. When wind in the sails caused his boat's ropes to strain, Ron was reminded of the sounds of the distressed towers, and he panicked. His brain was fractured.

"It's like someone has whacked you in the head with a baseball bat."

Ron was determined to dig his way out of this very black hole. A mortgage, his job, Monica, and Brigid were waiting at ground level.

"Brigid is incredible," says Ron. "She's very calm and quiet and angelic. She's a very good woman. She had a huge loss, too. Ruth was a great sister-in-law to her. And the fact that I was feeling the way I was became a loss for Brigid, too. It could never be the same again."

Ron says Brigid gave him the space he needed to grieve. She graciously managed the home front when Ron flew to Ireland to spend time with family.

"She was the perfect wife and the wife that Ruth said she would be." Ruth told Ron how she felt about Brigid when he began dating her. "She said, 'This is a special woman. She's gonna make a great wife.'"

They both shielded Monica from as much of the grief as possible. Ron says she was a well-behaved and loving daughter, and he stayed involved with all her activities. He also threw himself into work.

"Work was a huge distraction because I could roll up my sleeves, and I took a couple of companies that really needed me and brought them from zero to one hundred. I put my everything into it. It kept me busy, it kept me financially sound, it kept me going."

What did suffer was Ron's social life and various friendships. He found it uncomfortable and overwhelming to be around large groups of people or loud noises, like the explosion of fireworks on the Fourth of July. He avoided parties and the inevitable questions about how he was doing after 9/11. Ron also deliberately avoided soothing his pain with alcohol.

"I gave up drinking for the first three years," Ron says knowingly. "I didn't drink because I knew that if I jumped into a bottle, I'd pull the cork in after me."

Friends told Ron later that his humor was completely black for about five years. He even named his boat *Cruel Circus*.

Eventually, the intensive therapy and the support of his family helped Ron flush his poisoned subconscious. In the living room, he points to a colorful painting hanging on a wall behind me. He says it once served as one of several tools Dr. Doug gave him to cope with his emotions. The painting used to hang over the fireplace mantel where Ron could see it from the couch. Every day, he would look at the painting of rural Norway and imagine it was, instead, Ireland. The mental exercise transported him to a "happy place" where he could rest his weary mind. Ron also wrote down all of his bad dreams so he could talk through them in therapy sessions. Averse to flying following 9/11, Ron tackled his fear by riding in a friend's small plane and taking over the controls. Slowly, painfully, it worked. Seven months later, in the spring of 2002, Ron was able to fly to Cork to bury the remains of Ruth, which were recovered the previous December. (Juliana's remains were found in November 2002. She was buried next to Ruth in April 2003.)

Up to this point in our interview, Ron has not cried. He's been strong, but now we begin to talk about the very darkest days.

"That first Christmas was very hard," Ron says, choking back tears.

The families had traditionally gathered together for the holidays.

"I couldn't tell you how low I was. I was just"—his flat palm slices across the air—"the lowest I've ever been in my whole life." Ron stops talking and looks toward the front door with tears in his eyes. "The only mail that came on Christmas Eve was a letter from President Bush."

The letter, typed on official White House stationery, offered sympathies from the Bushes and thanked Ron for his "selfless efforts": *Your actions in the midst of this national tragedy were truly heroic. Your protecting and leading Jennieann Maffeo to safety as she struggled for her life reflected the best of the American spirit.*

The letter is not displayed in the house. Ron had to dig it out of an antique glass cabinet that Ruth gave him and Brigid as a wedding present. I ask Ron about his heroic act, not using that phrase. I ask him where the instinct came from to stay with Jennieann, a woman he didn't know, at a time when everyone else was running for their lives.

"People ran by us when I was in the lobby because they were just appalled and disgusted and horrified at the look of this woman," Ron says, placing his palm on his heart. "I mean, I was absolutely horrified as well, but I know from our Irish Catholic upbringing that you never leave someone in distress, that you are totally one hundred percent responsible for them until you can pass them on to the next medical station in life. That was ingrained in me growing up."

The years following the darkest days for Ron were filled with various business ventures and raising Monica. With donations that poured in from the States and Ireland, the family created the Juliana Valentine McCourt Children's Education Fund, a foundation to promote tolerance in children. Ron's mother, Paula, manages the six-acre McCourt Memorial Garden in Connecticut, officially opened in 2005, as a family tribute to Juliana and Ruth, who loved to garden.

In April 2006, Ron was asked by the Federal Bureau of Investigation to testify, along with thirty-nine other government witnesses, in the trial of Zacarias Moussaoui, accused of conspiring to kill

Americans in the 9/11 attacks. Ron says an FBI agent suggested he bring then-fifteen-year-old Monica to the trial in Alexandria, Virginia. Ron was skeptical, knowing that Monica never talked about 9/11 and that therapists told him to let her bring it up when she was ready. Monica was at least ready to listen. She was seated directly across from Moussaoui and, for the first time, heard her father's version of events that day.

Monica joins us in the living room. She shows me the special gift she received from Ron's mom for her recent twenty-first birthday: one of her aunt Ruth's rings, set with an aqua-blue stone. Monica also tells me about a family trip the summer before 9/11, when she enjoyed special treats from her aunt Ruth and time with her little "sidekick."

"Juliana was four and I was ten, so she would follow me everywhere. We slept in the same room," Monica recalls. "She would do everything I would do. If I said I didn't want eggs, she would say"—she crosses her arms in defiance like Juliana—"'I don't want eggs either.'"

Ron raises his eyebrows at me when Monica talks about her deceased aunt and cousin, as if to say, "Wow, she never does this."

Monica says she was interested in going to the Moussaoui trial to support her dad and to gain some perspective on an event that occurred when she was quite young. I ask her what she thought of her father's testimony.

"It was incredible." She pauses. "I didn't realize how close he was to the action. He was very brave."

For Ron, the trial provided tremendous relief; a hint of justice for his sister, niece, and all the victims; and an open door to more dialogue with his daughter.

"When we drove out of Alexandria that day toward home, I just thought, *My God, the cloud has lifted.*" Ron adds, "And I remember that was a huge moment. We had the trial, and this guy was found guilty."

Ron supports the life sentence for Moussaoui and the killing of Osama bin Laden, and he's eager for the government to push forward with the promised military trials for the remaining 9/11 terrorists held in the Guantánamo Bay detention camp.

"I'm adamant about having my day in court. These guys killed a lot of people, wrecked a lot of families, changed the face of America and the world. Every time I get on a plane I think about them. Every time I stand in a security line taking my shoes off I think about them. We've got to have some justice."

Sailing off the Irish coast. September 2011. (Courtesy of Ron Clifford)

Each year, on the anniversary of 9/11, Ron avoids all media coverage of the wretched morning. He chooses instead to spend the day sailing the Long Island Sound. There's always a special birthday gift for Monica that day, but she celebrates with friends on the weekend before or after the anniversary. My chat with Ron is one month after the much-anticipated ten-year anniversary, which he spent in Ireland with his brothers. The oldest, John, for the last ten years has housed the shard of glass the police officer brought to Ron from Ground Zero. The family decided to etch the infamous date on the glass and to pass it off to each other every ten years. The glass is supposed to spend the next ten years with Ron, but he says he couldn't bring himself to take the memento away from John's kids; it remains in Ireland. As we talk about his recent trip, Ron calls up several photos on his BlackBerry PlayBook; a new niece, Kayla Juliana, is a bright spot. The once-very-black humor is now simply healthy, as he points out a photo of an elaborate limestone headstone for Juliana and Ruth on the family plot in Cork. The sculptor has engraved the wrong birth date for Ruth.

"She'd *love* that!" Ron says with a grin.

As for the hallowed site here in the United States, Ron says he avoids Ground Zero. Friends visiting for Thanksgiving want to tour the new memorial and museum, but he won't join them. Ron says he makes a point of navigating around the area whenever possible.

"I got a flat tire on my way back from sailing several years ago right there. I thought," Ron laughs as if his sister was trying to get his attention, "*Ruth! Aw, Ruth!* I just felt like, *I gotta get the hell out of here.* I just don't feel good down there."

Ten years later, some residual angst still lingers in Ron's daily life. He's still startled by the explosive noise of his neighbor starting up his motorcycle. He continues to wake up from dreams where people jump off the Twin Towers. One element that's never been part of Ron's struggle is regret, and for that, he's grateful. He's made a point throughout his life of letting family and friends know how he feels about them. He didn't have the chance before his brother Gordon died, so, from that day on, and with Ruth's encouragement, he openly expressed his love for the people in his life. Ron says the loss of his father, sister, niece, and Paige would have been harder by tenfold if regret was added to the mix of pain and sadness.

"I think that's why people have a really bad time with some death and loss," Ron says, "because they haven't resolved any issues where they feel guilty. That's why you have to cherish people and don't go to bed feeling angry in your heart toward the one you love. Just figure it out. I have some very good friends, and even though we're guys, we tell each other we love each other. It's like, 'Love you, Jim,' you know? It's not being the least bit effeminate. You just have to tell people you care about them."

Ron has also found comfort in being grateful for his life, despite the losses. He loves the words a dear friend shared with him, a friend who's been battling cancer over the last few years. Ron says even through the rigorous regimen of treatments, his ill friend expressed gratitude.

"He had an exercise bike put next to his bed. He got out of bed in the hospital every morning and exercised, even as he was literally dying. One day he turned to me, and he wasn't a religious guy, but he turned to me and said, 'You know, if there's a heaven after this, it's a bonus.'"

As we wrap up the interview, Ron makes a point of telling me about the pretty houses along his street. He points to the left and encourages me, excitedly, to "go that way!" so I won't miss the sights. I'm amazed by this man's upbeat attitude and passion for life after all he's weathered. I tell Ron that people who read his story will want a magic bullet, his secret to coming out the other side of calamity with such a genuinely positive outlook on life.

"For me, would I like it to never have happened? Yes." He wipes his palms together back and forth in a washing-away motion. "But you gotta carry on with life. You can't just delay it. You can't feel sorry for yourself. Maybe you can for a month or whatever, but you gotta just hit it full blast. You just have to deal with things and try to think logically. Would this person who you lost want you to lose your life as a result of them losing theirs? I think no, they wouldn't." Ron ponders. "They'd want you to go forward."

Addendum

In May 2012, Ron had a home visit from Ed Ryan, one of the lead federal prosecutors in the upcoming death penalty case against alleged 9/11 mastermind Khalid Sheikh Mohammed and four accused coconspirators. Ryan and Ron have stayed in touch over the years, so Ryan knew that Ron and other victims' families were interested in their day in court.

"Having our day is a very good thing," says Ron. "I keep thinking of Lee Hanson, this guy in his sixties, and his wife. He wants the trial before he dies. His son and daughter-in-law and grandchild were on Ruth's plane."

Ron says his specific role in the proceedings is to share the trauma of not only escaping death himself but having to endure the sudden and tremendous loss of Ruth, Juliana, and Paige. The military trial will be held in Guantánamo Bay, where the suspects are imprisoned. Ron and anywhere from twenty to forty family members of victims will fly to the U.S. base in southeast Cuba to testify at the trial, its start date still to be determined. Ron will have several more visits with the Department of Justice to finalize the details of his testimony and what he might encounter during cross-examination.

"You can't forget those horrible details, y'know?"

I ask him if he needs to do anything to prepare for yet another unearthing of his buried anger and sadness.

"No, I think I'm emotionally there. I have often fantasized about killing the guy, y'know. I'm not that way, but when you start to read again about this maniacal nut who just orchestrated everything, the guy who held Daniel Pearl's head after he cut it off, when you read all the evidence against this animal, you start to get very, very angry that he could orchestrate a plan that did so much damage to our world."

The suspects will face charges including terrorism, hijacking, conspiracy, murder, and destruction of property. They could face the death penalty if found guilty. I ask Ron if he's on board with capital punishment for Khalid Sheikh Mohammed, for his role in the deaths of 2,976 people.

"Totally. Most definitely. I think this is one of the few times in life that you say, 'Look, there's so much evidence, he's admitted it, he doesn't deserve to live. He doesn't deserve to be part of this life.'" Ron continues, "It'll never be closure, but it will be a step to say, 'Yes, we went to court and the guy who was responsible for this, who crafted this, who put this together, who designed this, he's ultimately responsible and we have charged him, and he'll never see the light of day, or he'll get the death penalty.'"

Ron's not yet sure whether Monica or his youngest brother, Mark, will join him. He plans to use the challenging experience, as he has many times in his life, as another chance to learn and grow.

"It will be a good testament to how somebody gets tried under our constitution," he says, "and how the American justice system works for everybody, even people like him."

ROXANNE QUIMBY

Hiding in plain sight. That's how you could describe Roxanne Quimby's story when we found it. We were on the hunt for a rags-to-riches story, fascinated by people who had the drive and the perseverance to create something from nothing, and Roxanne's name popped up. Huh. How could we not already know this woman's name, like we do Sam Walton or Debbi Fields? Over the years, this masterful marketer has had no interest in promoting herself or her incredible story. Roxanne clearly wonders why someone would make a fuss about her journey. I love that about her. In Roxanne's mind, this life offers us the chance to dream it and do it. Why waste time talking about it? There are too many other things to accomplish.

◆◈◆

Roxanne Quimby was born in 1950 into middle-class comfort in Cambridge, Massachusetts, the oldest of three girls and a boy. Her father, a Harvard Business School graduate, sold large machinery to manufacturing companies and was always looking to expand his sales territory. The family moved every year or two to cities around the Northeast and Midwest. From a young age, Roxanne had an interest in not only creating things but peddling them, too.

"I was always selling stuff. I always tried to sell stuff to my sisters," Roxanne says with a laugh, "and to my parents. I'd bake muffins and go around the neighborhood and try to sell them to the neighbors."

When Roxanne was five, her dad made her a deal: he wouldn't give her money for college, but he'd match every dollar she earned herself. By the time she graduated from high school, Roxanne had saved $5,000, which her dad, as promised, boosted to $10,000. She enrolled in the University of Massachusetts, where she met a senior classman named George St. Clair who was studying comparative literature. They began dating, and after one semester, Roxanne became restless for a new view. The two headed west to Northern California. George had already graduated; Roxanne entered the fine arts program at the San Francisco Art Institute, where she studied oil painting. Once Roxanne got her bachelor of fine arts, she and George hit the road in search of a place to settle down. A place where trees were your neighbors.

"I had had it with big cities," she says, "and I knew I didn't want to live in the suburbs, so that was the only thing I hadn't tried."

Roxanne had also been influenced in college by the teachings of Helen and Scott Nearing, a husband and wife who wrote extensively about the art of simple, frugal, and purposeful living. At the peak of the Great Depression, the Nearings had moved from their small New York City apartment to a run-down farmhouse on sixty-five acres in rural Vermont and lived off the land.

"They were very inspiring because they had a lot of control over their own lives and their own destinies, and never had to punch a clock or answer to anybody but themselves," Roxanne explains, "and they lived with their values intact, raised all their own food, and were very independent."

In the summer of 1974, Roxanne and George set out in their

old Volkswagen van in search of cheap land. They soon realized they couldn't afford to buy in Northern California; there were no deals in Oregon or Washington, either. Hoping the opposite coast would prove more affordable, George and Roxanne drove the 2,200 miles to Vermont. Land there was too expensive, but rural northern Maine turned out to be right on the money. For $3,000, they bought thirty acres in Guilford, a small mill town fifty miles northwest of Bangor. With bow saws and a pioneer spirit, they cleared the land and built a two-room cabin and planted a vegetable garden.

"It was just trial and error," Roxanne says of the handiwork. "On-the-job training."

Roxanne's mother was supportive of her move to the woods, but her father was appalled.

"My dad had certain expectations about his children and how we would live our lives, and that was a real curveball. He never expected anything like that. He was very disappointed. His first reaction was, 'Wow, I wasted all that orthodontic work on you.' He spent so much money on braces when I was a teenager," she says with a chuckle, "and he thought I was moving to the tundra, where it didn't matter whether my teeth were straight or not."

Her father's displeasure with Roxanne's decision was rooted in more than just teeth. He felt a productive path in life must include an MBA and a substantial paycheck.

"That was how he evaluated our relationship: could he be proud of my achievements? And he defined them. He was not very proud of my living in the middle of the woods and clearly not pursuing any vocation that he could identify," she says, "and he just dropped me in a way."

It was the start of a father-daughter estrangement that would last for decades.

Roxanne and George set up camp in Guilford, sharing the woods with a few dozen like-minded families in a community known as back-to-the-landers. Each family built a home on a large piece of property and lived a subsistence lifestyle that rejected modern-day civilization.

"We spent most of our days outdoors, gardening, cutting firewood, hauling water, hiking, and camping," she says. "And that's what turned me into a real lover and appreciator of the outdoors."

In 1976, Roxanne and George married in his parents' backyard outside of Boston. All of Roxanne's family attended except for her father. The couple was content, and enjoyed the slow pace and self-reliance the rustic lifestyle offered.

"We had no electricity, so we tended not to stay up very late. There were no electric lights; we had kerosene lamps and candles. We didn't have television or any kind of media at night, so we'd read for a little bit and go to bed," she says. "We'd get up with the sun and we had a lot of daily chores to do. We didn't have running water, so we had to haul water from a spring; we chopped firewood to stay warm; we had a garden for our food; we had a woodstove to cook the food, so most of our day was consumed with these chores of eating and cooking and washing and hauling water and keeping firewood in the house. It was a pretty simple lifestyle."

The pair maintained a garden and stocked their root cellar, which substituted for a refrigerator. Once a month, a truck from Boston would drop off fresh food orders at the local co-op. Both worked odd jobs to pay the annual property taxes: Roxanne sold her art and waitressed, George worked as a disc jockey at the local radio station.

In 1978, they started a family. Roxanne gave birth at the local hospital to twins, Lucas and Hannah. Back at the cabin, Roxanne washed diapers in hot water boiled on the wood-burning stove and breast-fed the babies for six months.

Roxanne's twins Hannah and Lucas in a "stroller." Guilford, Maine, 1978.
(Courtesy of Roxanne Quimby)

"And then when they started eating solid food, I had a little baby grinder thing, this little crank-up thing," she says. "The Happy Baby grinder it was called, and whatever we were having, like rice or beans or potatoes, we put it right through the grinder and it would make a mash out of it."

No refrigeration required some creative cooking.

"We lived close by to a farm that raised chickens, so they always had a lot of eggs. They would have to grade their eggs by size, and any size that didn't fit the grader they would sell really cheap. They keep pretty well in a root cellar, so they'll last for quite a long time. So, I would get a lot of eggs and mix milk powder in them. They still hate that," she laughs, referring to the twins. "To this very day they won't eat it."

But the couple's once-simple lifestyle soon became quite complicated. Raising twins in the woods was a backbreaking challenge; there was no room for error. Their idealistic life had been hit with a double dose of reality.

"At first I embraced it all because I had chosen that lifestyle. I was a very conscientious environmentalist. I felt that when you haul water and you heat it up with wood that you've cut, dried, and hauled, you certainly don't waste water. You don't really waste anything. If you brought something in, it was through a lot of effort, and you used every bit of it. I remember buying old coats at the Goodwill and then cutting them down to make little jackets for my kids. We were just very conscientious, because we didn't have a lot of money and that was by choice. But by the time the kids were ready for school, it became very cumbersome to live that lifestyle, and I did start to get restless and feel that I just didn't think I was going to be able to do this the rest of my life. I had proven to myself that I could live that way, so I got a little bit restless and felt penned up."

By 1982, the back-to-the-land philosophy had created a back-to-the-wall lifestyle for the couple.

"It put so much pressure on our relationship. There was a lot of work to do. We had to carry everything into our cabin because it was a mile off of a dirt road. We had twins, and all of their clothing was washed by hand. We never had a telephone so we didn't feel we could leave our kids at home with a babysitter; our lifestyle just wasn't set up for that," Roxanne says. "We had very little money and we had to stretch it as far as it could go. We had lots and lots of chores and two babies, and the mounting responsibilities and hardships eventually became too much for the relationship to bear and I believe was a major reason why the marriage didn't last. I got married too young. I met George when I was nineteen and we lived together from then on, so I didn't have a lot of experience. By the time I was in my thirties I was like, *Wow, I wonder if he's really the right guy?*" She chuckles. "He was the first guy who came along. I should have waited a little bit longer and evaluated it."

In 1983, Roxanne told George she wanted a divorce.

"That wasn't so good. He was a lot more committed to the relationship," she admits. "He's not as much of a restless soul as I am and he was into a routine that suited him quite well, but I was just feeling bored and restless and I just needed more change, more variety, more stimulation in my life. So, I went out and pursued that, and he was pretty resentful that I had made a promise to be in a relationship till death do us part, and then I reneged on that promise; that did not go over well."

Roxanne packed up the kids and her belongings on a toboggan and pulled it to a nearby cabin owned by a friend who was living elsewhere for several years. The setup was just as rustic—no electricity or running water, a well, and a woodstove. She and George traded the kids each week.

"His fathering of our children was really great. They loved him," she says. "He's a very patient man, plays the guitar, he really loves them and spent a lot of time with them. They still have a very close relationship."

Despite the divorce, Lucas and Hannah embraced their down-to-earth upbringing in the woods. Dirt roads provided endless miles of bike trails.

"It was wonderful," says Lucas. "I grew up a very serious baseball fan and would often bungee-cord a transistor radio to the handlebars of my bicycle, and we would ride our bikes listening to Joe Castiglione, the Boston Red Sox radio announcer." He laughs. "We spent a lot of time doing that."

A nearby pond provided swimming in the summer and skating in the winter.

"I remember one ice-skating party we had with a bunch of different families and kids," Hannah recalls. "We spent a lot of time there."

In the community the twins called home, "modest" was mainstream.

"They took it as completely normal that they didn't have a TV and that we lived a very simple lifestyle," says Roxanne. "I think that, especially looking back on it now, they really appreciate how unique their life was growing up. We never had to warn them of the dangers of civilization and strangers and traffic and those kinds of issues you face when you're living in the city or suburbs. They had a very idyllic lifestyle. They could get on their bikes and go for the whole day. The only rule was that they had to come home before dark. So they would go pick apples and had a lot of freedom to go fishing or biking. One day they rode sixteen miles away and got a flat tire and had to deal with it." She smiles. "They had an old-fashioned childhood. I know when they look back on it now, they're very proud of the way they grew up and they tell their friends about it. It's a story they love to tell."

Alone with two children to raise, Roxanne began to worry about her paltry income stream. She was earning about $150 a week buying and reselling items at local flea markets. She continued to waitress but admits she was not cut out for the role of server.

"I had a real problem with asserting my independence," she says. "I was a very independent person. I had my mind made up about the way things were done, and I never failed to tell my boss what I thought they should do, and that didn't go over well. So, I ended up not being a very valuable employee because I was not very compliant."

There were three restaurants in Guilford, and Roxanne got fired from one. And then the next.

"They had started having this Thursday-night pizza night where it was all-you-could-eat pizza. They were trying to get people to come in during the week, and they only did it for four or five weeks in a row. They decided they didn't have the turnout they were expecting, and they stopped doing it. I remember telling my boss, 'You gotta keep after it a little bit longer than four or five weeks. It's gonna take a while for people to tell each other about it and for the word to spread. You gotta hang in there with it.' I look back now and think that was pretty inappropriate." She raises her eyebrows. "Telling my boss how to run her business. I'm sure she didn't appreciate it at all, but that's the kind of thing I would do."

When the kids started school, Roxanne began to notice that they felt self-conscious. She realized her personal choices were affecting the social status of the twins in their new environment.

"I was driving this old rickety van, and they would always ask me to drop them off about a block away from school so nobody would see the van that they were being dropped off in. Kids put a lot of pressure on each other, even at a very young age, to conform to society's standards, and it's a very unusual kid who can reject all those standards and just be happy for who they are, and I didn't want to put that pressure on my kids."

Financial pressure would soon mount for Roxanne; she lost her third and final waitressing job.

"I idolized Sinéad O'Connor. She shaved her head, so I thought I'd do the same. I went to work and they fired me on the spot." She laughs. "Once I became an employer and had my own employees, I look back on the situation and think, *Yeah, I would have fired me too!*"

Roxanne, now thirty-four, knew that her lifestyle had to change for the sake of her kids' future. The mainstream values she'd rejected began to make more sense when she saw them as a launching pad for Lucas and Hannah.

"I was concerned about the limitations that my choices were creating for them. They were going to this little school in northern Maine with an archaic social structure, not very enlightening, with a lot of emphasis on competition instead of cooperation, and I wanted to send them to an alternative school where kids were given more freedom to be themselves and be creative but couldn't afford to do that," she explains. "I eventually scraped together the money to get them there, but I realized as they got a little older that I was putting enormous limitations on the way they were going to be growing up because of choices I had made. The responsibility for their well-being motivated me to seek other ways of making a living that would allow me to offer them the opportunity for a better education, and for traveling, and to see the world more and understand it better."

Ironically, it was Roxanne's meager lifestyle that changed her world one afternoon. After the road-weary VW bus died, Roxanne had to walk or hitchhike to get around town. In the summer of 1984, a local character named Burt Shavitz noticed Roxanne's outstretched thumb and picked her up in his beat-up, bright yellow Datsun pickup truck. She knew him as a local beekeeper with a Howard Hughes–style reputation.

"Everybody had this notion that he was very wealthy, and yet he wore clothes that looked like he got them out of the bottom of a Salvation Army reject bag. His truck was a rattling can of nuts and bolts. He'd open the door and all kinds of stuff would fall out of it," she says, amused. "He set up his little honey stand on the side of the road and sat there in a lawn chair with his honey stacked up, sleeping, with the money jar set out if you wanted to buy some. He lived alone in this little turkey coop that he had salvaged, with his chickens and his horse. People were slightly afraid of him. He's kind of gnarly looking. He had a big, long beard and long hair. They'd make up stories about his life, like he was a millionaire from New York City who had come to Maine to hide."

Burt did indeed make his way to rural Maine from the big city.

Raised in Manhattan, he developed a love for photography and eventually made a living traveling and selling photos to national newspapers and magazines, including *Life* and *Time*. But in 1973, Burt tired of living out of a suitcase and in the chaos of a bustling city. He bought a twenty-acre farm in the small town of Garland, fifteen miles south of Guilford. He fixed up an eight-feet-by-eight-feet turkey coop discarded by a neighbor and called it home. He bought fifty beehives, scattered them across the countryside, and earned about $3,000 a year selling honey on the roadside in nearby Dexter.

"I was completely fascinated by him," Roxanne says. "He was so odd and unusual and independent. I was really inspired by the fact that he was not willing to compromise in any way whatsoever. He knew what he wanted, he didn't care what anybody thought about it, and I found that very inspiring."

And quite attractive. Roxanne was not only romantically interested in the forty-nine-year-old, but as a gardener, she was intrigued by his honeybees. She spent the summer of 1984 learning beekeeping from Burt, and before long, Roxanne realized she could add value to Burt's substandard business. He was packaging his honey in used pickle jars.

"People called him Dirty Burty. You would really kind of wonder whether you really wanted to eat that honey or not." She chuckles. "It had no shelf appeal whatsoever. So, I had an art background, and I felt that if I had the opportunity to put the honey into more interesting packaging with more interesting labels, we could sell it for more, and we would both be able to make a living at it. So, I suggested that to him and he was fine with it. He's kind of a lazy guy." She smiles. "Y'know, *Never do anything yourself that you can get somebody to do for you.* He said, 'Sure, Roxy.' He called me Roxy. 'You go for it, Roxy.'"

Roxy ditched the pickle jars and packaged the honey in charming teddy bear and hive-shaped containers. Business got sweeter, but the love affair would eventually sour.

"He's a confirmed bachelor, and he's not really equipped to have a relationship." She pauses. "Um, a two-way relationship. He didn't have a lot of emotional vulnerability and he's kind of closed off, and after a while it was pretty clear it wasn't going to work."

Burt, Roxanne, Rufus. Moosehead Lake, Maine, 2000.
(Courtesy of Roxanne Quimby)

But it was very clear that the business could. Roxanne and Burt agreed to continue their work relationship. A breakthrough came one day as they wandered into the honey house.

"He sold the honey, which was pretty easy; you just bottle it. But he never really figured out what to do with the wax, so he just kept it in the honey house. It's wonderful stuff, beeswax. It's fragrant and gorgeous, and he suggested that I make some candles. 'Why don't you make some candles with all this wax, Roxy?' So, I was like, *Yeah, this is like sculpture! This is very artistic and a lot of fun!* It was sort of an epiphany that we could use this wax, and as soon as we used up all the wax he had on hand, we started buying wax from the other beekeepers who were in the same boat." She adds, "No one ever knows what to do with the beeswax."

They struck up a deal: Burt would keep the bees and gather the honey; Roxanne would package the golden treat and make the candles. She bought wicks, drew bees and hives on labels, and experimented with various molds.

"It was trial and error. I'm not really afraid of failure because it usually leads to understanding something that you didn't know before."

The local junior high Christmas craft fair and bake sale would be their first shot at selling the handcrafted products; a vendor table cost five dollars. Game on.

"We made two hundred dollars that day," she recalls, "and I was really psyched, because that was a lot of money at the time for me."

Burt and Roxanne pooled their funds to buy basic kitchen appliances for mixing, pouring, and dipping. They traveled to craft fairs around the region, and Roxanne set a goal of $20,000 in sales for the first year. That number would mean $10,000 in profits, tripling her current income. Roxanne was exhilarated by the promise of a brighter future for her children and a creative challenge for herself.

"I just unleashed this energy that I didn't even know I had," she says. "I was thrilled with the packaging of the honey, designing labels and hang tags, taking it out to the craft fairs, and making candles with the beeswax. I just loved this little craft business that we had going, and Burt was fine with it, like, 'Yeah, I don't have to sell honey by the side of the road anymore. I can sleep in my own cabin instead of in a lawn chair in the middle of town,'" she mimics, laughing.

Over the years, Roxanne traveled to the majority of trade shows solo, and George would watch the kids. She'd set out at midnight in her old pickup or van and arrive in the morning to avoid paying for a hotel room. Sometimes she slept in the truck. When the twins were around seven years old, Roxanne started taking them along to weekend shows.

"It was like these little adventures every weekend," says Lucas. "We would pile up the car with candles and honey and get to go to a place where there were a bunch of people. It was always exciting because there were so many people around."

Hannah remembers looking forward to heading out in the early-morning darkness, knowing a special treat was in store at the first gas station or drive-through.

"I can remember stopping one time and getting McDonald's or Burger King, or someplace we would never go, and I got French toast sticks." She giggles. "I can remember so clearly sitting in the back of the van and eating my French toast sticks."

Roxanne says, "They looked forward to that because it was a trip into civilization. It was very exciting for them. They used to tell me that they were old enough to make change, and then at the trade shows they would try to convince me they were old enough to take orders. They would be highly insulted if I would take the pen away and tell them *I* was writing the orders."

Roxanne traveled to larger and larger craft fairs around the region, and before long, to the big city of Boston. Daily retail sales grew from hundreds of dollars to more than a thousand. In an effort to expand the limited product line, Roxanne began to explore additional items she could make with beeswax, like polishes. On her tiny cabin's wood-burning stove, she brewed batch after batch of shoe and furniture polish. Craft fairs served as the company's research and development department.

"I didn't participate in the marketplace very much because I was broke; I didn't buy anything. I didn't think I was a consumer myself," she reasons, "so they were almost sort of an alien species and I was watching them very carefully. It was obviously very important to me to understand what made people buy things. I watched them to see what motivated them to purchase something or when they decided not to buy something. Why didn't they? I listened very carefully to people who were there with their friends to see what they said to each other, and I would watch their actions. One of the things I noticed was that everybody would pick up a candle, turn it over, and look at the underside of it for some reason. I don't know why, but I always made sure the bottom of the candle looked as good as the top."

Before long, it was time to add square footage. Burt and Roxanne convinced a friend to rent them his abandoned schoolhouse for the price of the annual fire insurance: $150. The building had plenty of critters but no running water or electricity. Still, it was an upgrade in terms of space and allowed them to hire several employees to help meet the growing demand. They installed a gas kitchen range and worked at night by the light of kerosene lamps. Although she was working around the clock, Roxanne was extremely engaged.

"I think I was a born merchant. I just really was fascinated by the whole thing about selling stuff. Making stuff and selling stuff. It really caught my interest, and once I started doing it as an adult I was really into it."

Hannah says her mom's laser focus on developing the business didn't interfere with family time; it actually enhanced it.

"For a long time, I would say until we got to high school, we were very much a part of it," Hannah says. "When we were younger, we were going to the trade shows and the craft fairs, and we were helping. We probably saw more of our mom than most kids did, because we were helping wrap soap and packaging things up, and doing a lot of that with her. She was working nonstop, but there was this blurred line of what was work and what we were doing as a family."

The passion and hard work was paying off. Not only had they met the first-year goal of $20,000, by 1987 retail sales reached $81,000. From day one, Roxanne made sure the freedom and independence she valued as a person were intrinsic in their business plan.

"The company grew without debt. All the sales that we made were reinvested in growing the company, and because we had no debt, we had no one that we needed to explain our business strategy to," she says. "We never had to pay back any loans or interest, which is very liberating because you don't have a bank or a lender second-guessing your every move. And if we made a mistake we paid for it, so you learn really fast."

In an effort to reduce drive time to countless retail craft fairs, Roxanne shifted their sales effort to the wholesale market. In 1989, the move paid off in a big way. At a wholesale show in Springfield, Massachusetts, a buyer for an upscale Manhattan boutique named Zona ordered several dozen teddy bear candles. When he put the products in the store window, they were a hit. The Fifth Avenue boutique reordered hundreds of candles, and several big chains followed suit: Gardener's Eden, Smith & Hawken, and the Smithsonian Museum Store. Roxanne knew it was again time to move. Corporate headquarters became an abandoned bowling alley in the middle of Guilford.

"It was bigger than the schoolhouse, and it had electricity and running water," she says, "so that was a major step forward."

Forty employees joined the effort and annual sales reached

$180,000. Production was under way in several outbuildings as well.

"We burned down a place, and fortunately, no one was hurt. But five thousand pounds of honey were burned up. We had honey all over the bottom of a burning building, like six inches thick, with burning timbers falling into it. It was a whole year's worth of honey and we stored it in five-gallon plastic buckets," she recalls, "so, of course they all melted in the fire and all the honey came seeping out. The fire truck finally got there and the firemen turned on the hose and went sliding around in all the honey. They finally put it out, but we lost all the honey."

Despite the setback, Roxanne forged ahead, searching again for additional ways to entice consumers. She found a treasure trove of ideas in the pages of antique farm manuals Burt had collected.

"Many farms back in the 1800s had bees, just like they'd have chickens for eggs, a couple of cattle, and a couple of hives of bees for honey," she explains. "They would have these farm journals, talking about the best way to grow rutabagas and the rest of it. And Burt had them; he had found them. They were beautiful antiques with these gorgeous engravings, and there was a recipe for everything in there. And one of the recipes was for lip balm, and I tried that recipe, and I started enhancing the recipe with medicinal herbs that I grew. I started tinkering around with the recipe and came up with lip balm, and it was just a winner. People really loved it. It felt good on their lips, it worked really well, and it was a home run. But, I must say, I had about fifty 'outs.'" She laughs. "I had about fifty products that didn't sell well before I had one that sold very well."

Roxanne added an image of Burt's unique face to the product labels. She had met an artist named Tony Kulik at a craft fair in Maine and fell in love with his etchings and art. She asked him to create a woodcut of Burt's face and also beehives. The process involves carving a reverse image into a block of wood. The artist carves carefully, making sure the printable parts remain level with the surface and the non-printable parts are chipped away.

"He would send me the actual woodblock that was carved, and he would also send an image of the carving and send it on a piece of paper," she explains, "and we would send it to the printer. It retained its woodcut look, which is a very old-fashioned technique."

The combination of quirkiness on the outside, and wholesome beeswax and sweet almond oil on the inside, made the lip balm a huge success. It was also a conclusive hint from consumers about what they wanted to buy.

"Everybody who came into the booth would buy a lip balm, but very few would buy furniture polish. It was trial and error. And I would later learn that personal-care products sell better than candles for sure. So, creams and balms and lotions that are made with a beeswax base outsold candles and honey enormously. Eventually, we just completely dropped the honey and candles," she says, chuckling, and adds, "and furniture polish."

When sales in 1991 hit $1.5 million, Roxanne and Burt incorporated the company. Burt owned one-third of the shares, Roxanne two-thirds. She was raising two children and was more committed to the business and to nurturing its growth. They were producing half a million candles a year, as well as natural soaps and perfumes cooked up on gas stoves. Two years later, they moved yet again, to an old house, where they manufactured seventy-five different products. Roxanne's emphasis on using natural ingredients and packaging responsibly was simply an offshoot of her personal philosophy about clean eating and respecting the environment.

"I felt that one of the biggest problems with personal-care products was that they created an enormous amount of waste with the packaging, and they were full of chemicals that were basically not very good for your skin. I was eating organic food, and I had a garden, and I understood, 'Garbage in, garbage out.' You really want to have a good, healthy diet, and you want to have natural products on your skin, and I wasn't going to try to convince consumers otherwise. I felt that it was a story that people needed to hear, that whatever you put on your skin, basically you're eating it. It ends up in your body and your bloodstream, and it either nourished your body or your body had to rid it of toxins. We did that by using ingredients that most people could find in their kitchen. Very simple ingredients, very nourishing ingredients, like avocado and coconut. It's all kind of cliché now, but at the time, there weren't that many companies doing it," she says. "You could read the ingredients on the back of the jar and pronounce every one of them, and the story that was being told was that this product was really good for your body, and I think it really resonated with consumers."

She admits her marketing plan is well defined in hindsight, but at the time, she was simply letting consumer behavior reinforce her business decisions.

"Looking back, the world was getting very, very complicated. So, having a product that was so simple was kind of reassuring to people. It was like an 'Oh, whew!' Y'know, just like a comfort food: comfort cosmetics. The other thing that was very attractive to people was that a lot of the other personal-care companies used incredibly gorgeous women to sell their products, women who were flawless. And that set a very high expectation for women," she says, "and most of us don't measure up in that way. But by using this hippie, bearded, long-haired Jerry Garcia guy as our spokesperson, we eliminated that expectation about beauty, and we always made the claim that beauty comes from within; it's how you feel and what you eat and how you live and how you act—that's real beauty, not what you look like. And so we told that story, and since 90 percent of our customers were women, many of them really liked hearing that. They were really ready to hear that. Now, there were some people who would write to us like, *How could you put that filthy, dirty hippie on the jar?*" She laughs. "But other people would be like, *Thank you for letting me not have to look like America's top model and I can still feel okay.*"

By 1993, their personal care products were sold in every state in the nation and annual sales reached $3 million. The company had nearly fifty people working in production facilities in Guilford and nearby Cambridge. But square footage once again reared its squashed head; a major expansion was needed to fill all the orders. And that's when a queen-bee moment for Roxanne presented itself. She'd learned from beekeeping that, ultimately, every move made by honeybees is for the good of the hive, even if it means kicking out lazy drones in the dead of winter. Survival of the hive ruled. Roxanne knew the company had reached a point where future growth would be hampered by two realities in Maine: payroll taxation and Guilford's location.

"There was not the labor pool we needed. It's way off the beaten track. There was no way for me to set up a shipping system and there weren't any bookkeepers or accountants around, the kind of professional people I needed to run a company," she explains. "The first bookkeeper we had, he had to drive about seventy miles in both directions to get to Guilford. It was just against the odds. We interviewed people who would come up from Portland, Maine, or Boston and they'd say, 'I'd love to work for you, but I could never convince my family to move up here.' So, we decided the way to grow the company was to leave Maine."

It was a difficult decision for Roxanne. The women working for her were previously unemployed moms. She'd be leaving behind friends, the community, and her roots. But Roxanne knew that the company had huge potential for growth and that she needed help to foster it. She called Burt and told him of her plan. He said, "Okay, Roxy."

"He's not an artistic guy; he is not an ambitious guy," she says of Burt. "He never had this burning need to prove anything to anybody. He really didn't care what anybody thought about him. I remember one day someone came into the booth and asked if our candles came in smaller sizes and he said, 'Yeah, just break 'em in half.' He didn't have a lot of customer service or marketing sensitivities. But on some level he gave me an enormous amount of support without trying to; he just was kind of like a rock. He was always there. I knew I could lean on him pretty hard and he'd never fall over. He was sort of a north star in a way."

Over the next ten years, the stars would align for Roxanne in a dazzling display of accomplishment.

TEN YEARS LATER

In April 2012, my in-person interview with Roxanne, set for her home in Florida, fell through because she was instead in Portland, Maine, where she lives several weeks a year and runs the Quimby Family Foundation, a nonprofit organization focused on the environment and the arts. We instead talked over the phone. Like bees that dart back and forth to the same flower, certain buzzwords returned repeatedly to our conversation: "freedom," "restlessness," "independence." Similar phrases appear in Roxanne's quotes when you read about her: "black sheep," "outlaw at heart," "queen bee." This is not a woman you get to know by peeling back layers; Roxanne has no peel. She is self-aware, direct, and as open as the millions of acres of Maine forest that feed her soul.

In 1994, ten years after Roxanne met Burt, the queen bee picked up the hive and headed for business-friendly North Carolina. Taxes would be lower and the level of skilled labor would be higher. They leased a former garment factory in Creedmoor, twenty miles north of Raleigh-Durham, a hub of cosmetics manufacturing. The company was selling fifty products, some distributed as far away as Japan. The master plan was to automate manufacturing and to recruit a seasoned management team.

I wondered if Roxanne, now making big strides toward becoming a "player" in personal-care products, had made contact with her estranged father. Wouldn't he be proud of her tenacity and success? She told me no, he never called her. But Roxanne said her mom shared with her that he'd read a December 1993 issue of *Forbes* magazine featuring a story about her business acumen.

"Someone told me that he was running around the post office in his little town, 'That's my daughter! That's my daughter!' Also, Harvard had done a case study on the company, and he reads the Harvard newsletter or magazine that they send out to their alumni," she says, "so he got letters from his old classmates saying, 'Hey, I read about your daughter in the business review,' and he was like, 'You gotta be kidding me!' So, it kind of blindsided him. It was weird for him. My sisters both had MBAs and he had an MBA from Harvard, and he felt we should all get MBAs and follow a career path that led to financial success, which is why he was so upset with me when I went to art school, like, 'You're not gonna get anywhere that way.' And so it was very strange for him that he would encounter my story in a business magazine of all places."

Another man in her life who was experiencing the strange and weird was Burt. He went to North Carolina to help relocate the company but felt unsettled from the start. Roxanne watched her friend struggle to navigate life where the trees part and the pavement begins. Within weeks, Burt moved back to his converted turkey coop in Maine.

"He was not well equipped for modern-day civilization," she describes. "He kept getting lost in the parking lot; he could not find his car. He just wasn't a city guy. He was good enough to help set up the company, but I think he only stayed six weeks and then he went back to Maine. It was pretty clear he wanted to leave. I think the thing that was the straw that broke the camel's back was when the Department of Agriculture came in on a routine inspection and told him he was not allowed to bring his dog, Rufus, to work. And that was it for him."

Roxanne's twins, at seventeen, were enjoying boarding school in western Maine, giving her time to commit to the business. She was burning the beeswax candle at both ends. Factories for Almay, the Body Shop, Pond's, and Revlon were within twenty miles, so Roxanne jumped at an invitation from a factory manager at one of the large, multinational cosmetics companies to go on a tour.

"I went over there and it was just mind-boggling. I think it was a million square feet and it was an incredible, high-tech place. One of the things he said was that out of every dollar they sold their product for, twenty-five cents of it went into advertising and eighteen cents of it went into the jar. So they were actually spending more money selling the product than they put in the jar. I was flabbergasted by that, because our little tagline, where it shows a picture of Burt, says, *We put the beauty in the product, folks. We have to*. Sort of like, 'We don't have it on the box; we have it in the jar.' And what we did to get the word out was make these tiny sample packs of our product, and we'd give them away," she says. "Burt would go to one of our stores, like one of the Whole Foods stores, and he'd give out signed, autographed T-shirts and samples of our lotions and lipsticks. People would try them, and if they liked them they would buy the full-size product. We relied on word of mouth instead of advertising, and that's how we kept our prices very reasonable."

Roxanne hired a plant manager from Revlon and a sales and marketing manager with experience at Lancôme, Vogue, and Victoria's Secret. She also added highly skilled managers in the shipping and finance departments.

"I surrounded myself with people who had skills that I did not have," she explains. "I tend to be artistic and creative and experimental and I'm kind of disorganized. My desk in my office is a complete wreck and I have to be really messy, and I surrounded myself with people who are very orderly and very disciplined. I had a great engineer running the plant, I had a great chemist running the lab, I had a great IT person running our accounting department; I had really good people at what they did. I never hired real creative types." She laughs. "We had that. I had tons of MBAs working for me, and I love MBAs because they're so organized."

While Burt, the unconventional face of the product, continued to make store appearances several days a month, Roxanne was in charge of every dollar and every product. In 1998, with $8 million in annual sales and a new life a thousand miles from home, Roxanne had a moment. For the first time, she allowed herself to take her eyes off the road ahead and sneak a look in the rearview mirror. She was all alone in the one-hundred-thousand-square-foot production warehouse.

"It was quite late at night. Everybody had left, and for some reason I needed something out in the warehouse," she recalls. "I went out to the warehouse from my office and started walking back to the shipping area, and I was looking at these racks, and I thought, *Wow! I just can't believe this!* It looked like a great big old factory, and

I just had this moment when I just stood there and looked at it, like *When did this all happen? Where did this all come from?* And I felt at that moment that we had kind of turned a corner, and we were now a mainstream company with departments, and we had a couple hundred employees and a lab. We were getting pretty sophisticated in the way we were doing things, and at that point I felt quite gratified that we had taken it out of a little kitchen and put it into a mainstream factory."

The wonder of all she'd achieved made Roxanne sentimental. In the days ahead, she picked up the phone and called her father, whom she hadn't spoken to in decades.

"I felt like, *I'm probably the one who should call him because I'm younger and have more flexibility and he's kind of stuck in his ways, and I'm just going to reach out.* He was very happy that I had. He was very proud, and I don't think he knew how to bridge the gap," she says, "but when I reached out to him, he was really happy that I did."

Roxanne says that she never tapped into the pain caused by the rift in their relationship; she instead used it as a motivator.

"I tend to move on and take my lumps. I don't tend to dwell on the upsets of life, but on some level I think my ambition was a way of proving to myself and proving to him that he was wrong about me," she says. "And it could have been that if he'd been more accepting of me all along, I wouldn't have had this need to prove anything to him or myself, so in some ways I was clearly affected by his hard-line approach."

By 1999, annual sales approached $14 million, and products became readily available with the launch of an e-commerce website. Roxanne was weary of life away from her beloved Maine, so she moved back to the coastal lobster village of Winter Harbor and bought a 1,600-square-foot house on the rocky shore. She also bought the adjacent lot for privacy. E-mail and overnight shipping allowed her to oversee the company from afar, with bimonthly visits to North Carolina. Roxanne made the company her own the same year; she bought out Burt's one-third share. The buyout came in the form of a trade. Roxanne bought Burt a $130,000 house in Maine, which he sold just a few months later and returned to his treasured turkey coop. The next year, revenue soared to $23 million and Roxanne began to receive offers to sell the company. She wasn't ready yet but knew the day would, and should, come.

"I knew it was just a phase in my life, not my life," she says, "and so I ran the company as if it were the last product I would sell. I positioned it in a way that would make it very attractive to an acquiring firm. I had a bottom line that was very attractive; good, steady, healthy growth; I never took a lot of money out; I never cooked up any fiction with the books—it was just really solid."

While she continued to grow the company, Roxanne began to consider how her mounting profits could honor her environmentally conscious customers and her love of nature. In 2002, Roxanne established Elliotsville Plantation, a private operating foundation for the acquisition and conservation of thousands of acres of wild land in northern and coastal Maine.

"Buying all the land that we bought felt like I was still serving our customer," she says. "I had taken the profits that all of our customers had allowed us to earn and was investing it for them."

As Roxanne managed the large-scale success of the company, she also navigated the similarly sized business challenges. One involved the delivery of more than a half million dollars' worth of face cream to a major national retail chain. After the shipment was made, Roxanne received a call from the chain's warehouse manager. Blue mold was growing on the top of every single jar.

"Their chemist was just quality-controlling it before they sent it out to their stores. It was devastating. It wasn't just the fact that we had six hundred thousand dollars' worth of product that was molding; it was a credibility issue, too. We were incredibly embarrassed.

This was a major chain and here we had completely disappointed them and we looked really bad," she says. "It turned out to be a natural preservative we were using, and the company that made the preservative had moved from one factory to another and had used a new source of water in their manufacturing process, which had some kind of different formula than their old water, and it created this problem for us. We had to take the blame because it was our problem. It's our name on the jar. That was humiliating and devastating and it made us feel horrible, but we kept soldiering on. It's not like you can just quit. I had a little saying on my office wall that said, *Success is going from one failure to the next.* These kinds of things happen all along the way, from the very beginning, like when you run out of gas before you get to the craft fair and you miss the first three hours of the day because you miscalculated, all the way up to having hundreds of thousands of dollars of product go bad in a major customer's warehouse. There are lots of setbacks."

That same year, with sales topping $60 million, Roxanne hired a female business broker and began entertaining offers from New York equity companies. Her plan was to sell the majority of her shares but to also keep some.

"I was feeling my creativity was being compromised, because a lot of my time was being spent as a manager instead of as an artist, managing a lot of people, a lot of meetings, and I just was feeling really limited and I was just restless," she explains. "I wanted to try something new. I had proven to myself that I could do it, so that thrill was over. I just felt it was time for someone else to take over."

Roxanne knew that as a minority owner she would be vulnerable, so she wanted to make sure she had a strong feeling about the firm she ultimately chose as the buyer. A student of metaphysics since she was nineteen, Roxanne did tarot card readings on each suitor. She paired the guidance of the universe with her own instincts.

"I rely on it, especially with things that I don't know enough about. I had my gut feelings about who I trusted and who I didn't. But then, when I had an angel card or a tarot card that affirmed my gut feelings, then I would feel like, *Check! Okay, that's another check.*"

The angel card came up for a private equity firm out of New York called AEA Investors. *Check!*

In 2003, AEA paid Roxanne $141.6 million for an 80 percent stake in . . . *drumroll, please* . . . Burt's Bees.

Yep. The company Burt and Roxanne started in 1984 was named after the words Burt stenciled on each of his hives: BURT'S BEES.

"I always thought it was so funny, like, these are Burt's bees, like, they know it. 'Oh, yeah, we're Burt's, not someone else's,'" Roxanne says, chuckling. "It was easy to remember. I started putting it on the labels, and I would push them toward people as they walked by the booth and they would all want to say," she singsongs, "'Burt's Bees! Burt's Bees!' There was something kind of fun about that name, so it stuck."

When Roxanne made the AEA deal, Burt asked Roxanne for money, since he'd traded his shares years earlier for a home. She agreed to pay him $4 million.

"And I'll bet he hasn't spent a penny of it. I'm sure it's all under his mattress or hiding under his dog food bowl." She laughs. "He hasn't changed a bit. He's still living out in that little shack that he lives in. I haven't seen him for a year or two. He had a fight with the phone company over his bill, so they disconnected his phone, so now you can't even call him anymore. He's just really eccentric."

Burt did invest in some home improvements. He expanded his turkey coop from eight feet by eight feet to eight feet by twelve feet. He also bought a classic motorcycle.

"And it was a used motorcycle, and it wasn't running when he bought it." With a laugh she says, "It took him about three years down at the shop to get the thing working again. That's how he spends his days, fixing lawn mowers that don't work. Stuff like that."

Roxanne admits she and Burt have grown apart but that she could find him at any time, and they are friends.

After the first selloff, Roxanne still owned a 20 percent share in the company. She also retained a seat on the board of directors; she knew a second sale would come in the years ahead.

"I wanted to be sure I had at least some input, and I wanted to keep my ears open and meet with the people who were running the company and owned the majority," she says. "Y'know, kind of protecting the investment that I had and watching over what they were doing with it."

In 2004, Roxanne used half of her Burt's Bees shares to form the Quimby Family Foundation, a nonprofit organization that supports fellow nonprofits of like mind. The forest and the arts would be the benefactors; the tax shelter was gravy.

"Because it was a nonprofit, it was not a taxable transaction, which was fabulous, because that was a lot of money that would have had to have been paid in taxes," she says, "so I was able to shelter quite a bit of money from taxes by creating this nonprofit, and that allowed me to take up a social mission, and the mission was the environment."

Lucas and Hannah, at twenty-six, joined the foundation's board of directors in 2005.

"Oh, yeah, they love it. They feel very important," she says through a smile, "and they truly are."

Roxanne's entrepreneurial burnout didn't last long. In January 2006, she founded Happy Green Bee, a company that manufactures all-organic clothing for children and babies. One of the collections is called "Oxanna," Russian for Roxanne.

The final sale of Burt's Bees came in November 2007. Potential buyers swarmed and made offers, eager to grab market share in the lucrative "green" products sector. AEA sold Burt's Bees to Clorox for

$925 million. Roxanne's remaining 20 percent share netted her close to $183 million. The unemployed mom who realized she wanted more for her kids had banked a whopping total of $325 million.

I ask Roxanne if she ever envisioned that large a payday in her wildest dreams.

"Never, no, never. It's strange. I just had a very indifferent attitude about money because I had always understood way back when that it didn't buy happiness, it couldn't buy you peace of mind, it couldn't buy you love, it couldn't buy you the most important things, which is why I moved to the country and lived such a simple life," she says. "I think my indifference to money allowed me to make decisions that were not based on emotions, so those decisions were better. If you're making decisions based on fear, or want, or greed, or pride, or some of the other things that accompany money, your decisions are compromised by those emotions, and you don't make the clearest, best decisions that you could. I didn't have a lot of emotions attached to money; it was just there. I didn't covet it or fear that it would go away, or that I wouldn't have enough."

Roxanne viewed the dollars as a pat on the back, not as a way to pad her wallet.

"I never really was all that interested in money for what it could buy. The money for me was more like the score, and business was the sport," she says. "I prided myself on playing the game well and the skill was measured by dollars. The money I was able to make by selling the company was more like gratification that I had done a good job as opposed to, *Oh, good. Now I can go out and buy stuff.*"

Lucas says his mom instilled the same view of money in him and Hannah. Their lifestyle never changed even as the company grew. Boarding school was the big splurge. Lucas says his mom, while she values education, has never lost sight of the learning that takes place on a hiking trail, rock wall, or trip across the globe.

"She's given us amazing opportunities, but it's always really focused," he says. "It's never like, 'Hey, y'know what? You should have a Maserati,' or 'Here's a bunch of money to go do something.' It's always, 'Let's go as a family to Africa,' and we would experience that culture, and it was an amazing thing that we'll always remember as a family."

Roxanne has traveled to Hawaii and Antarctica and all the places she's always wanted to go. She studied at Le Cordon Bleu in Paris and bought multiple homes in Florida and Maine. But the majority of "stuff" Roxanne spends her millions on is acreage. For years, she's been purchasing large tracts of forestland in northern Maine with the ultimate goal of creating a new national park. She hopes to give the National Park Service seventy-four thousand acres of her northern Maine woods to create the Maine Woods National Park. Her donation would ideally fall on the Park Service's centennial anniversary in August 2016. Roxanne's dream is not shared by all. Her land acquisition is not popular with many hunters, loggers, and outdoorsmen who fear their freedom to work and play may be compromised by the creation of a national park. Her mission is a work in progress.

Not surprisingly, Roxanne is sought after as a public speaker. Her story is so compelling that she's frequently asked to share her "secrets" of success. When she speaks to young people interested in starting companies, she's direct.

"Very rarely are you gonna have a home run right out of the box. You're gonna go through a lot of trial and error, you're going to make a lot of mistakes, and you're gonna have a lot of things that don't sell. And the major thing is not to be discouraged," she advises, "because you learn so much more from your mistakes than you do from your successes, and as long as you're making mistakes you're probably on the road to success. You're learning what doesn't work, and you're refining your vision."

Now sixty-two years old, Roxanne is still as busy as a bee. She spends as much time as she can with family. Her mother has passed away, but her father, who's almost ninety, lives in Florida with his girlfriend. Roxanne says he's had three failed marriages, one that lasted just six months.

"Now he's decided that he's had such little success with marriage that he'll just have a girlfriend instead," she says with a laugh, "so he lives with his girlfriend who's ninety-one."

Hannah, Lucas, Roxanne. Maine, 2011. (Courtesy of Roxanne Quimby)

Lucas and Hannah are now thirty-three. Both have hiked the Appalachian Trail and paddled the Northern Forest Canoe Trail. Lucas lives in Seattle with his wife and fourteen-month-old daughter Gabriella. He works full-time with the Quimby Family Foundation and part-time as a fly-fishing guide. He's a graduate of Le Cordon Bleu cooking school in London and worked in the food and wine industry for more than a decade. I ask Lucas if he ever buys Burt's Bees products.

"Yeah," he says with a laugh, "I got a tube of lip balm in my pocket."

Hannah lives in San Francisco and works part-time with the foundation. She has a degree in human development and photography, as well as a master's degree in integrative health. She's now pursuing certifications in holistic nutrition and personal fitness. She'd like one day to share her love of the outdoors by running a nonprofit organization that would make health and wellness more accessible to adults and children. Hannah, too, still uses the products that decades ago she and her brother watched bubble on the kitchen stove.

"Even when I went to college it really wasn't even known then; just by people who shopped in health food stores or who bought natural products," she says. "But now I'm in class and I'll see someone pull it out and use it and I'll think, *That is so crazy*. It's all around me now, and I have a clear memory of wax melting on the woodstove and what it used to be, and to think it's become what it has still surprises me sometimes."

The twins have maintained a close relationship and see each other every few months.

"I just want them to be happy and fulfilled and do right," Roxanne says of the twins, "and to live according to the values I hope I instilled in them. And to be honest with themselves and others. That's what I want for them."

Perhaps surprisingly, knowing all Roxanne has accomplished, she considers her most stunning achievement a 2010 summit of Mount Katahdin, Maine's highest mountain.

"You can't have anybody do it for you," she says. "You can't hire a really great engineer to do it for you. You gotta do it yourself, and it's tough. For me, it was really challenging. I'm not the best hiker in the world and it was always very intimidating for me. I felt like, *Aw, I can't do it. It's too high and I'm not strong enough. It's too scary. It's too steep.* So when I got to the top I felt like, *Wow! I did it!* It was just a really great feeling. I had to do it on my own. That's why I felt it was such a great achievement for me."

It's that can-do spirit that Roxanne talks about passionately when I inquire about the message of her journey so far. Those same buzzwords hum behind her answer: "freedom," "restlessness," "independence."

"This country is still great enough that you can make it no matter what. I was not trained to be a Wall Street wizard. I didn't know anything about business. I didn't have any financial leverage or advantages. I was a woman, and yet, even with those obstacles, I was allowed to be successful in this country. For me, this country gives us enough freedom and enough opportunity that a person can still make it," she says. "My mother was born in a different country, and my grandfather was born in Russia, and his father and sister were murdered one night because they were Jewish. He ran away from Russia and he went to China and got married and they had to leave China during the Communist revolution, and they left with nothing. So in our family, there was always this story about America, and how no one would be persecuted for their religion, and that this was the land of opportunity, and I really believe in that. I know we're not perfect and I know there are problems in our society, but I still feel like there's a lot of opportunity in this country to succeed and to dream and to aspire."

I'll never again see a Burt's Bees display without thinking of Roxanne. And Burt, happily cooped up. Every Walgreens, Target, and

Walmart carries Burt's Bees, and the product line continues to grow. I ask Roxanne her gut reaction when she walks by the brand during her daily doings.

"I sort of feel like it's overexposed right now. When something gets overexposed it doesn't seem quite as special, quite as unique," she says. "I controlled the marketing of it a little more strictly, but obviously, the people who own it now want to sell it to every single company they can, so they do. I don't know, once in a while I have a little glimmer of, *Oh, yeah. I did that.* I remember one day I was taking a hike somewhere, and I saw this little yellow piece of litter in the mud. It was a used-up Burt's Beeswax Lip Balm, and I had a little moment there, thinking that this product was so ubiquitous that it was now litter." She laughs. "It was like a Coke can on the side of the road, and I thought, *Wow! I've really made it in America.*"

Boy, have you ever, Roxy.

Addendum

How's Burt doing? The mystique continues. Burt declined an invitation to be interviewed for the story. A little bee told me he was headed to Taiwan soon for a company appearance. He's apparently a rock star in East Asia. All the best to you, Burt, and your bees.

CONCLUSION

In 1988, Stan Sandroni hired me after twenty-seven other television news directors turned me down for my first job out of college. I never dreamed I would be rejected so many times; I never thought I'd live and work in Greenville, Mississippi. But that chance meeting with Stan gave me the start I needed to develop a solid career. In 1998, ten years after Stan gave me my first reporting job, NBC called and offered me a position as a correspondent for *Dateline NBC*. I've been working for the network in New York ever since. That fateful day when I met Stan taught me that one person can change your life. If just one person believes in you, the army of people who don't are inconsequential. All you need is someone to take a leap of faith, and your world can change. That road trip also proved to me that persistence pays off. When you're worn out and feel like you have nothing left in the tank, you most likely do. I say stick fatigue, rejection, and doubt in the trunk and hit the gas one more time. Your Stan could be right around the corner.

My game changer isn't nearly as dramatic as the ones described in the stories you've just read. The game changers for Amy, Lindsay, Patrick, Diane, Ron, and Roxanne all required guts and the determination to not only survive, but to also accept the scars and welcome the lessons that followed. Does that mean they are different people ten years later? After all, chaos and adversity are often catalysts for great change. Ron knows something about that. Then again, one brave step followed by a second can also blaze a trail to change, if we're patient enough to go the distance. Just ask Amy. Sometimes we seek out change, other times it finds us and demands our attention. Can people really change? And if so, does the change stick around for good?

Here's what they think:

Amy Barnes—survived domestic abuse and lost 340 pounds
"You *can* change but you have to want it badly enough. I tell my clients every day, 'I will give you every tool I have in my brain and in my heart that I used to lose weight, that I used to survive my relationship and become a survivor, and that I use in life in general. I will give you absolutely every tool, but I can't want it badly enough for you. You have to want it yourself.' If you really want to change who you are for the better, it definitely takes time. It doesn't happen overnight."

Lindsay Beck—fought for her life and her dream to have a family
"Cancer absolutely changed me. I used to joke that it sparked my 'quarter-life crisis.' Seniors often say they wish they knew then what they know now. In a lot of ways, I think cancer gave me that gift at a very young age, and I've had the privilege to live my life with that perspective. There are daily habit changes, like eliminating as many toxins as possible from my environment by using natural cleaning products and eating organic. There are also deep changes, like the drive to live an extraordinary life. I do wonder, though: Did cancer do this to me or would I have come to it anyway? I don't have answers, but I know that who I am today is very different from who I was before cancer."

Patrick Weiland—lost a sister to domestic violence and overcame drug addiction

"If I hadn't changed I'd be dead. There's no question. So, can people change? Yes. Can you wake up one day and change? No. It's a very incremental process and I think it's one that's so mystifying. Even with the murder of my sister, it took me a year and three months until I was able to stop using. So, there are moments that are wake-up calls for us, but it's our decision whether we listen, our willingness to change our thinking. I do think it's a myth that we can change ourselves alone, as an island, by ourselves. We need the people who are close to us, the people in our lives who love us and the people we love, in order to change. They're the ones. It's with their help."

Diane Van Deren—elite ultra runner who underwent brain surgery following a decade of seizures

"Did it change who I am and how I think about life? No. But it made me stronger, it made me more stubborn, it elevated my perseverance. That's what it did. Now I can encourage change. I can have an impact. What I've been through has given me an opportunity to make change by having a voice and sharing what I've learned."

Ron Clifford—survived the 9/11 attacks but lost his sister, niece, and family friend

"I didn't die there. I wasn't killed there. I made it out alive, so my life *had* to change there. The change is I'm loving life a lot more. I'm treasuring life a lot more. I love the small things. I love the big things. I love life. Before, I was more concerned with work and putting the bacon on the table and paying the mortgage. Now I just take a deep breath and think, *Oh my gosh, look at that seagull. Look at that magnificent landscape over there.* I appreciate life a lot more."

Roxanne Quimby—from organic rags to riches

"I see our life on earth and all of creation as evolving toward enlightenment and perfection. In order to realize progress on the path, we have to let go and keep moving forward. Evolution is managed change rather than random change. I think both kinds are fun and keep life interesting!"

My hope is that this book offers you a sense of peace about the future and the power we all have to shape ours. Each of the six people you've met never imagined what a decade would mean to their journeys; they focused instead on soldiering through each day. Now, looking back, they are grateful and empowered, and most importantly, passionate about living their next ten years to the fullest. May you be inspired to embrace the what-ifs in your life, to trade your fears for faith. Take a chance, push through indecision, celebrate the unknown, and always believe in a bright future. It's possible, no matter how impossible it may seem at any given moment.

ACKNOWLEDGMENTS

My thanks and a huge hug:

To Jon Karp, who walks around all day with a lightbulb over his head that blinks bright ideas. They never stop and they always give you goosebumps.

To my editor, Marysue Rucci, for her wise eyes and enduring spirit. How did you help me give birth to my book at the same time you were on bed rest, nurturing the little girl inside of you? Rock star. And to Marysue's right (and left) hand, Emily Graff. Super star.

To the movers in publicity: Tracey Guest, Jessica Zimmerman, and Rebecca Marsh. And the shakers in marketing: Andrea DeWerd and Richard Rhorer.

To Megan Kopf, a master juggler, who somehow planned her wedding at the same time she was "getting me to the church on time" for the whirlwind of publicity. You deserve two honeymoons.

To my agent, Mel Berger, who is always there when I need him and who I'm always glad to see, even when I don't need a thing.

To the book's six superstars who make my challenges look like blessings: I am in awe of your strength and courage. Each of you let me drag you back to the dark days, over and over again, as I checked off my endless list of questions. You went there repeatedly with grace and patience and for that I am grateful. Amy, Lindsay, Patrick, Diane, Ron, and Roxanne: You are gems. What an honor to mine your stories.

And to Time. Without you, we'd all be stuck wondering instead of arriving at the glorious other side of *what if.*

I've saved the best for last. To Jane Lorenzini, who not only has a gift, she *is* one. Janie can string together four words and instantly move you. But beyond being an exceptional writer, she is an even better friend. I am lucky.

ABOUT THE AUTHOR

Hoda Kotb was named coanchor of the fourth hour of *Today* in August 2007. She has also been a *Dateline NBC* correspondent since April 1998 and is the *New York Times* bestselling author of *Hoda: How I Survived War Zones, Bad Hair, Cancer, and Kathie Lee*. In her years at NBC, Hoda has covered a wide variety of domestic and international stories and has received numerous awards, including the 2008 Alfred I. duPont–Columbia University Award and the prestigious Peabody in 2006. The three-time Emmy winner also won the 2003 Gracie Award and the 2002 Edward R. Murrow Award. She resides in New York City.

ABOUT THE COAUTHOR

Jane Lorenzini is a freelance writer and coauthor of *The New York Times* bestseller, *Hoda: How I Survived War Zones, Bad Hair, Cancer, and Kathie Lee*. A professional writer for nearly three decades, Jane enjoyed a fifteen-year career as a television news anchor and reporter. She also designs and manufactures her own line of stationery products called *plain jane*. She lives in Tennessee.

Share your own inspiring *Ten Years Later* story at
www.TenYearsLaterBook.com or by emailing
TenYearsLater@simonandschuster.com.